The European Union: A Very Short Introduction

'John Pinder has for years been recognized and respected as an outstanding authority on European Community, now European Union affairs. This short, detailed yet splendidly readable book . . . is a must for anyone seeking to understand the European Union, its origins, development, and possible future.'
Michael Palliser

'John Pinder writes straightforwardly and beautifully clearly . . . He has done an extraordinary job of compressing the history and the book is absolutely up to date.'
Helen Wallace, Sussex European Institute

'John Pinder is in a class of his own. He brings clarity and vision to what is too often complicated and obscure. He causes both friend and foe to wonder what a reformed and strengthened Union could achieve for all Europe and for the wider world.'
Andrew Duff, MEP, Constitutional Affairs Spokesman, European Liberal Democrats

. . . indispensable not only for beginners but for all interested in European issues. Pithy, lucid and accessible it covers recent history, institutions, and policies, as well as future developments.'
Rt. Hon. Giles Radice, MP

'it not only lives up to but exceeds the promise of its title. This is in fact "The European Union – A Very Short, Useful and Straightforward Guide".'
Independent on Sunday

'invaluable'
William Keegan, *Observer*

VERY SHORT INTRODUCTIONS are for anyone wanting a stimulating and accessible way in to a new subject. They are written by experts, and have been published in more than 25 languages worldwide.

The series began in 1995, and now represents a wide variety of topics in history, philosophy, religion, science, and the humanities. Over the next few years it will grow to a library of around 200 volumes – a Very Short Introduction to everything from ancient Egypt and Indian philosophy to conceptual art and cosmology.

Very Short Introductions available now:

ANCIENT PHILOSOPHY
  Julia Annas
THE ANGLO-SAXON AGE
  John Blair
ANIMAL RIGHTS   David DeGrazia
ARCHAEOLOGY   Paul Bahn
ARCHITECTURE
  Andrew Ballantyne
ARISTOTLE   Jonathan Barnes
ART HISTORY   Dana Arnold
ART THEORY   Cynthia Freeland
THE HISTORY OF
  ASTRONOMY   Michael Hoskin
ATHEISM   Julian Baggini
AUGUSTINE   Henry Chadwick
BARTHES   Jonathan Culler
THE BIBLE   John Riches
BRITISH POLITICS
  Anthony Wright
BUDDHA   Michael Carrithers
BUDDHISM   Damien Keown
CAPITALISM   James Fulcher
THE CELTS   Barry Cunliffe
CHOICE THEORY
  Michael Allingham
CHRISTIAN ART   Beth Williamson
CLASSICS   Mary Beard and
  John Henderson
CLAUSEWITZ   Michael Howard
THE COLD WAR
  Robert McMahon

CONTINENTAL PHILOSOPHY
  Simon Critchley
COSMOLOGY   Peter Coles
CRYPTOGRAPHY
  Fred Piper and Sean Murphy
DADA AND SURREALISM
  David Hopkins
DARWIN   Jonathan Howard
DEMOCRACY   Bernard Crick
DESCARTES   Tom Sorell
DRUGS   Leslie Iversen
THE EARTH   Martin Redfern
EGYPTIAN MYTHOLOGY
  Geraldine Pinch
EIGHTEENTH-CENTURY
  BRITAIN   Paul Langford
THE ELEMENTS   Philip Ball
EMOTION   Dylan Evans
EMPIRE   Stephen Howe
ENGELS   Terrell Carver
ETHICS   Simon Blackburn
THE EUROPEAN UNION
  John Pinder
EVOLUTION
  Brian and Deborah Charlesworth
FASCISM   Kevin Passmore
THE FRENCH REVOLUTION
  William Doyle
FREUD   Anthony Storr
GALILEO   Stillman Drake
GANDHI   Bhikhu Parekh

Available soon:

For more information visit our web site

www.oup.co.uk/vsi

John Pinder

THE EUROPEAN UNION

A Very Short Introduction

OXFORD
UNIVERSITY PRESS

OXFORD

UNIVERSITY PRESS

Great Clarendon Street, Oxford OX2 6DP

Oxford University Press is a department of the University of Oxford.
It furthers the University's objective of excellence in research, scholarship,
and education by publishing worldwide in

Oxford New York

Auckland Bangkok Buenos Aires Cape Town Chennai
Dar es Salaam Delhi Hong Kong Istanbul Karachi Kolkata
Kuala Lumpur Madrid Melbourne Mexico City Mumbai Nairobi
São Paulo Shanghai Taipei Tokyo Toronto

Oxford is a registered trade mark of Oxford University Press
in the UK and in certain other countries

Published in the United States
by Oxford University Press Inc., New York

British Library Cataloguing in Publication Data

Data available

ISBN 13: 978- 0-19-285375-2
ISBN 10: 0-19-285375-9

9 10

Typeset by RefineCatch Ltd, Bungay, Suffolk
Printed in Great Britain by
Ashford Colour Press Ltd, Gosport, Hants.

Contents

Foreword

Some say it was Shaw who apologized for writing a long letter
because he hadn't time to write a short one, some say Voltaire.
Doubtless both did. They might have said the same about writing a
book. I should have thought of that when Shelley Cox of OUP invited
me to write this *Very Short Introduction*. I have written much on the
subject but without the tough constraint that this implies; and the
need to explain a complex entity so succinctly presented a challenge
that I found hard to meet.

The core of the problem is to concentrate on the essentials. I have been
following the development of the Community, now the Union, since its
inception half a century ago, and acquired a large stock of facts and
ideas from which to choose what seem to be the most relevant for this
book. I soon formed the view that it would be best to move by steps and
stages in a federal direction and have since seen no reason to change it.
This does not mean pulling up the old nations of Europe by the roots
and trying to plant them again in virgin soil, but developing a
framework in which they can deal with their common problems in an
effective and democratic way. My choice of ideas is inevitably coloured
by this view. But my concern has been to present them in a way that will
help to provide a context for reasonable people, whether they lean
towards a federal or an intergovernmental approach, to evaluate the
performance of the Union and judge in which direction it should go, at a

time when critical choices affecting its future will have to be made. And I have endeavoured to be scrupulous about the facts.

In seeking, as something of a generalist, to be accurate about the range of the Union's affairs, I have been greatly helped by people with special knowledge of the several subjects covered in the book. My thanks are due in particular to Iain Begg, Andrew Duff, Nigel Haigh, Christopher Johnson, Jörg Monar, and Simon Nuttall. Simon Usherwood has assisted invaluably with boxes, charts, chronology, glossary, and maps. Shelley Cox and her colleagues have combined efficiency with understanding of an author's needs. I have relied, as ever, on Pauline Pinder's wise advice. If what follows does not please the reader, it is no fault of theirs.

The Treaty of Nice

On 10 December 2000, shortly before this book was due to go to press, the European Council concluded the Treaty of Nice. This will change the working of the Union's institutions in some significant ways; so in order to make the text as up to date as possible, Oxford University Press has enabled me to make appropriate revisions, though necessarily within strict constraints of time and space. Some of the changes are due to come into affect in 2005, others when the Treaty has been ratified by all member states, probably in 2002 at the latest. Until then, the existing treaty provisions prevail.

J.P.
December 2000

Abbreviations

ACP	African, Caribbean, Pacific countries
AFSJ	Area of Freedom, Security and Justice
Benelux	Belgium, Netherlands, and Luxembourg
CAP	common agricultural policy
CE	compulsory expenditure
CFC	chlorofluorocarbon
CFSP	Common Foreign and Security Policy
CIS	Commonwealth of Independent States
CJHA	Co-operation in Justice and Home Affairs
CO_2	carbon dioxide
Comecon	Council for Mutual Economic Assistance
Coreper	Committee of Permanent Representatives
EAGGF	European Agricultural Guidance and Guarantee Fund
EC	European Community
ECB	European Central Bank
ECJ	European Court of Justice (formal title, Court of Justice)
Ecofin	Council of Economic and Finance Ministers
Ecosoc	Economic and Social Committee
ECSC	European Coal and Steel Community
ecu	European Currency Unit (forerunner of euro)
EDC	European Defence Community
EDF	European Development Fund
EEC	European Economic Community

EEA	European Economic Area
Efta	European Free Trade Association
EMS	European Monetary System
Emu	Economic and Monetary Union
EPC	European Political Co-operation
ERDF	European Regional Development Fund
ERM	Exchange Rate Mechanism
ESCB	European System of Central Banks
ESF	European Social Fund
EU	European Union
eua	European Unit of Account (forerunner of ecu)
Euratom	European Atomic Energy Community
euro	replaces the currencies of most member states in 2002
Gatt	General Agreement on Tariffs and Trade (forerunner of WTO)
GDP	Gross Domestic Product
GNP	Gross National Product
GSP	Generalized System of Preferences
IGC	Intergovernmental Conference
Nato	North Atlantic Treaty Organization
NCE	non-compulsory expenditure
NTBs	non-tariff barriers
OECD	Organization for Economic Co-operation and Development
OSCE	Organization for Security and Co-operation in Europe
PHARE	Poland and Hungary: aid for economic reconstruction (extended to other Central and East European countries)
QMV	qualified majority voting (in the Council)
SEA	Single European Act
TACIS	Technical Assistance to the CIS
TEC	Treaty establishing the European Community
TEU	Treaty on European Union
UN	United Nations
VAT	value-added tax
WEU	Western European Union
WTO	World Trade Organization

List of boxes

List of charts

List of illustrations

List of maps

Chapter 1
What the EU is for

The European Union of today is the result of a process that began half a century ago with the creation of the European Coal and Steel Community. Those two industries then still provided the industrial muscle for military power; and Robert Schuman, the French Foreign Minister, affirmed on 9 May 1950 in his declaration which launched the project that 'any war between France and Germany' would become 'not merely unthinkable, but materially impossible'.

A durable peace

It may not be easy, at today's distance, to appreciate how much this meant, only five years after the end of the war of 1939–45 which had brought such terrible suffering to almost all European countries. For France and Germany, which had been at war with each other three times in the preceding eight decades, finding a way to live together in a durable peace was a fundamental political priority that the new Community was designed to serve.

For France the prospect of a completely independent Germany, with its formidable industrial potential, was alarming. The attempt to keep Germany down, as the French had tried to do after the 1914–18 war, had failed disastrously. The idea of binding Germany within strong institutions, which would equally bind France and other European countries and thus be acceptable to Germans over the longer term, seemed more promising. That promise has been amply fulfilled. The French can regard the European Community (EC) and now the European Union (EU) as the outcome of their original initiative, which became the central project of their European policy. The French have at the same time sought, with considerable success, to play the part of a leader among European nations. But participation in these European institutions on an equal basis has also given the Germans a framework within which to develop peaceful and constructive relations with the growing number of other member states.

For Germans, following the twelve years of Nazi rule that ended with devastation in 1945, the Community offered a way to become a respected people again. The idea of a Community of equals with strong institutions was attractive. Schuman had also declared that the new Community would be 'the first concrete foundation of a European federation which is indispensable to the preservation of peace'. But whereas French commitment to developing the Community in a federal direction has been variable, the German political class, having thoroughly absorbed the concept of federal democracy, has quite consistently supported such development. In 1992, indeed, an amendment to the Basic Law of the reunited Germany provided for its participation in the European Union committed to federal principles.

The other four founder states, Belgium, Italy, Luxembourg, and the Netherlands, also saw the new Community as a means to ensure peace by binding Germany within strong European institutions. For the most part they too, like the Germans, saw the Community as a stage in the development of a federal polity and have largely continued to do so.

Although World War Two is receding into a more distant past, the motive of peace and security that was fundamental to the foundation of the Community remains a powerful influence on governments and politicians in the six founder states. The system that has provided a framework for half a century of peace is regarded as a guarantee of future stability. A recent example was the decision to consolidate it by introducing the single currency, seen as a way to reinforce the safe anchorage of the potentially more powerful Germany after its unification; and in the coming period there will be continuing pressure to strengthen the Union's institutions in order to maintain stability as eastern enlargement increases the number of member states towards thirty or more, including at least a dozen new democracies. The focus on the economic aspects of integration that has been common among British politicians has diverted attention away from this underlying motive and restricted their ability to play an influential and constructive part in such developments.

Economic strength and prosperity

While a durable peace was a profound political motive for establishing the new Community, it would not have succeeded without adequate performance in the economic field in which it was given its powers. But the Community did in fact serve economic as well as political logic. The frontiers between France, Germany, Belgium, and Luxembourg, standing between steel plants and the mines whose coal they required, impeded rational production; and the removal of those barriers, accompanied by common governance of the resulting common market, was successful in economic terms. This, together with the evidence that peaceful reconciliation among the member states was being achieved, encouraged them to see the European Coal and Steel Community as a first step, as Schuman had indicated, in a process of political as well as economic unification. After a false attempt at a second step, when the French National Assembly failed to ratify a treaty for a European Defence Community in 1954, the six founder states proceeded again on the path of economic integration. The concept of the common market was extended to the whole of their mutual trade in goods when the European Economic Community (EEC) was founded in 1958, opening up the way to an integrated economy that responded to the logic of economic interdependence among the member states.

The EEC was also, thanks to French insistence on surrounding the common market with a common external tariff, able to enter trade negotiations on level terms with the United States; and this demonstrated the potential of the Community to become a major actor in the international system when it has a common instrument with which to conduct an external policy. It was a first step towards satisfying another motive for creating the Community: to restore European influence in the wider world, which had been dissipated by the two great fratricidal wars.

The British, who had not suffered the shock of defeat and did not share

1. Churchill at The Hague: founds the European Movement, following his call for 'a kind of United States of Europe'

the conviction that there must be radical reform of the European system of nation-states, stood aside from the Community in the 1950s. With some exceptions, they failed to understand the strength of the case for such reform. One such exception was Winston Churchill who, less than a year and a half after the end of the war, said in a speech in Zurich: 'We must now build a kind of United States of Europe . . . the first step must be a partnership between France and Germany . . . France and Germany must take the lead together.' But although few among the British understood so well the case for a new Community, many were reluctant to be disadvantaged in Continental markets and excluded from the taking of important policy decisions. So after failing to secure a free trade area that would incorporate the EEC as well as other West European countries, successive British governments sought entry into the Community, finally succeeding in 1973. But while the British played a leading part in developing the common market into a more complete single market, they continued to lack the political motives that have driven the founder states, as well as some others, to press towards other forms of deeper integration.

It is important to understand the motives of the founders and of the British which, while they continue to evolve, still influence attitudes towards the European Union. Such motives are shared, in various proportions, by other states that have acceded over the years; and the dozen or more that can be expected to join in the next decade or two will bring their own mixtures of motives, including a strong desire among most of them to join the European mainstream after their long period of exclusion under Soviet domination. These differing varieties of political and economic motives underlie much of the drama that has unfolded during the last fifty years, to produce the Union which is the subject of this book.

Theories and explanations

There are two main ways of explaining the phenomenon of the Community and the Union. Adherents to one emphasize the role of the member states and their intergovernmental dealings, adherents to the other give greater weight to the European institutions.

Most of the former, belonging to the 'realist' or 'neo-realist' schools of thought, hold that the Community and the Union have not wrought any fundamental change in the relationships among the member states, whose governments continue to pursue their national interests and seek to maximize their power within the EU as elsewhere. A more recent variant, called liberal intergovernmentalism, looks to the play of forces in their domestic politics to explain the governments' behaviour in the Union. For want of a better word, intergovernmentalist is used below for this family of explanations as to how the Community and Union work.

One should not underestimate the role that the governments retain in the Union's affairs, with their power of decision in the Council that represents the member states and their monopoly of the *ultima ratio* of armed force. But other approaches, including those known as neo-functionalism and federalism, give more weight than the intergovernmentalists to the European institutions.

Neo-functionalists saw the Community developing by a process of 'spillover' from the original ECSC, with its scope confined to only two industrial sectors. Interest groups and political parties, attracted by the success of the Community in dealing with the problems of these two sectors, would become frustrated by its inability to deal with related problems in other fields and would, with leadership from the European Commission, press successfully for the Community's competence to be extended, until it would eventually provide a form of European governance for a wide range of the affairs of the member states. This offers at least a partial explanation of some steps in the Community's development, including the move from the single market to the single currency.

A federalist perspective, while also stressing the importance of the common institutions, goes beyond neo-functionalism in two main ways. First, it relates the transfer of powers to the Union not to a spillover from existing powers to new ones, but to growing inability of governments to deal effectively with problems that have become transnational and so escape the reach of existing states. Most of these problems concern the economy, the environment, and security; and the states should retain control over matters with which they can still cope adequately. Secondly, whereas neo-functionalists have not been clear about the principles that would shape the European institutions, a federalist perspective is based on principles of liberal democracy: in particular, the rule of law based on fundamental rights, and representative government with the laws enacted and the executive controlled by elected representatives of the citizens. In this view, the powers exercised jointly need to be dealt with by institutions of government, because the intergovernmental method is neither effective nor democratic enough to satisfy the needs of citizens of democratic states. So either the federal elements in the institutions will be strengthened until the Union becomes an effective democratic polity, or it will fail to attract enough support from the citizens to enable it to flourish, and perhaps even to survive.

Subsequent chapters will try to show how far the development of the Community and the Union has reflected these different views. Meanwhile the reader should be warned: this writer considers that the need for effective and democratic government has moved the EC and the EU by steps and stages quite far in a federal direction and should, but by no means certainly will, continue to do so.

Chapter 2
How the EU was made

'Europe will not be made all at once, or according to a single, general plan. It will be built through concrete achievements, which first create a de facto solidarity.' With these words, the Schuman declaration accurately predicted the way in which the Community has become the Union of today. The institutions and powers have been developed step by step, following the confidence gained through the success of preceding steps, to deal with matters that appeared to be best handled by common action.

Subsequent chapters consider particular institutions and fields of competence in more detail. Here we see how interests and events combined to bring about the development as a whole. Some primary interests and motives were considered in the previous chapter: security, not just through military means but by establishing economic and political relationships; prosperity, with business and trade unions particularly interested; protection of the environment, with pressure from green parties and voluntary organizations; and influence in external relations, to promote common interests in the wider world.

With the creation of the Community to serve such purposes, other interests came into play. Those who feared damage from certain aspects sought compensation through redistributive measures: for France, the common agricultural policy to counterbalance German industrial advantage; the structural funds for countries with weaker economies, which feared they would lose from the single market; budgetary adjustments for the British and others with high net contributions. Some governments, parliaments, parties, and voluntary organizations have pressed for reforms aiming to make the institutions more effective and democratic. Against them have stood those who resist moves beyond intergovernmental decision-making, acting from a variety of motives: ideological commitment to the nation-state; a belief that democracy is feasible only within and not beyond it; mistrust of foreigners; and simple attachment to the status quo. Among them have been such historic figures as President de Gaulle and Prime Minister Thatcher, as well as a wide range of institutions and individuals, most prevalent in Britain and Denmark. Among the European institutions, it is the Council of Ministers that has come closest to this view.

Two of the most influential federalists, committed to the development of a European polity that would deal effectively with the common interests of the member states and their citizens, have been Jean Monnet and Jacques Delors. Both initiated major steps towards a federal aim. Altiero Spinelli represented a different kind of federalism, envisaging a European federal constitution achieved at one stroke. The German, Italian, Belgian, and Dutch parliaments and governments have in varying degrees been institutionally federalist, as have the European Commission and Parliament, and, in so far as the treaties could be interpreted in that way, the Court of Justice. They have generally preferred Monnet's stepwise approach, although the Italians and Belgians, and at times the European Parliament, have espoused constitutional federalism.

1950s: the founding treaties

Monnet was responsible for drafting the Schuman declaration, chaired the negotiations for the ECSC Treaty, and was the first President of its High Authority. These two words reflected his insistence on a strong executive at the centre of the Community, stemming from his experience as Deputy Secretary-General of the interwar League of Nations which convinced him of the weakness of an intergovernmental system. He was, however, persuaded that, for democratic member states, such a Community should be provided with a parliamentary assembly and a court – embryonic elements of a federal legislature and judiciary – and that there should be a council of ministers of the member states.

This structure has remained remarkably stable to this day, though the relationship between the institutions has changed: the Council has become the most powerful; the European Commission, while still important, has lost ground to it; the European Parliament has gained in power; and the Court of Justice has established itself as the supreme judicial authority in matters of Community competence. Although they were later to accept these institutions, British governments of the 1950s felt them to be too federal for British participation.

2. Founding Fathers: Monnet (left) and Schuman (right).

3. Page one of the text Monnet sent to Schuman for his Declaration of 9 May 1950

The six member states, however, were minded to proceed further in that direction. The French government reacted to American insistence on German rearmament, following the impact of communist expansionism in both Europe and Korea, by proposing a European Defence Community with a European army. An EDC Treaty was signed by the six governments and ratified by four of them; but opposition grew in France and the Assemblée Nationale voted in 1954 to shelve it. Perhaps this was just as well, for the Community institutions, even if strengthened by a treaty for a European Political Community that had also been prepared, were probably not strong enough to bear such a heavy responsibility. The result was that the idea of a competence in the field of defence remained a no-go area until the 1990s.

The Treaties

Rome wasn't built in a day; and the Treaties of Rome (in force in 1958) were a big building block in a long and complicated process that has constructed the present European Union. Other major treaties include the ECSC Treaty (in force 1952), Single European Act (1987), Maastricht Treaty (1993), Amsterdam Treaty (1999), and Nice Treaty (concluded by European Council in December 2000).

A minor complication is that there were two Treaties of Rome (see below), but the EEC Treaty was so much more important than the Euratom Treaty that it is generally known as *the* Treaty of Rome.

A major complication is that the European Union was set up by the Maastricht Treaty, with two new 'pillars' for foreign policy and internal security alongside the European Community, which already had its own treaties. These have been consolidated in the EC Treaty (TEC), which continues to exist alongside the EU Treaty (TEU) though the EC is an integral part of the EU. So there are now two Treaties, closely linked and with common institutions, though the Court of Justice, the Commission, and the European Parliament play a more important role in the EC than in the other two pillars.

NB: to avoid undue complexity, this book follows two principles in referring to the EC and EU:
- **European Community, Community, or EC is used regarding matters relating entirely to the time before the EU was established, or after that time if the EC's separate characteristics are relevant;**
- **European Union, Union, or EU in all other cases.**

While the collapse of the EDC was a severe set-back, confidence in the Community as a framework for peaceful relations among the member states had grown; and there was a powerful political impulse to 'relaunch' its development. The Dutch were ready with a proposal for a general common market, for which the support of Belgium and Germany was soon forthcoming. The French, still markedly protectionist, were doubtful. But they held to the project of European unification built around Franco-German partnership and so accepted the common market which the Germans wanted, on condition that other French interests were satisfied: an atomic energy community in which France was equipped to play the leading part; the common agricultural policy; the association of colonial territories on favourable terms; and equal pay for women throughout the Community, without which French industry, already required by French law to pay it, would in some sectors have been at a competitive disadvantage. The Italians for their part, who had the weakest economy among the six, secured the European Investment Bank, the Social Fund, and free movement of labour. So all these elements were included in the Rome Treaties, which established the European Economic Community (EEC) and European Atomic Energy Community (Euratom): an early example of a package deal, incorporating advantages for each member state, which has characterized many of the steps taken since then.

The two new treaties entered into force on 1 January 1958. Euratom was sidelined by de Gaulle, who became President of France in the middle of that year and was determined to keep the French atomic sector national, in the service of French military power. But the EEC became the basis for the future development of the Community. Its institutions were similar to those of the ECSC, though with a somewhat less powerful executive, called Commission instead of High Authority; and the EEC was given a wide range of economic competences, including the power to establish a customs union with internal free trade and a common external tariff; policies for particular sectors, notably agriculture; and more general co-operation.

4. De Gaulle says 'non' to Britain.

5. Thatcher says 'no' to the single currency.

The first President of the Commission, Walter Hallstein, was a very able former professor of law and convinced federalist who, as a senior figure in Chancellor Adenauer's government, had been Monnet's principal partner in negotiating the ECSC Treaty. He led the Commission into a flying start, with acceleration of the timetable for establishing the customs union; and within this framework the Community enjoyed notable economic success in the 1960s, with growth averaging some 5 per cent a year, twice as fast as in Britain and the United States. But conflict between the emergent federal Community, as conceived by Monnet or Hallstein, and de Gaulle's fundamentalist commitment to the nation-state made that decade politically hazardous for the Community.

The 1960s: de Gaulle against the federalists

In June 1958, less than six months after the Rome Treaties came into force, de Gaulle became French President. He did not like the federal elements and aspirations of the Community. But nor was he prepared to challenge directly treaties recently ratified by France. He sought, rather, to use the Community as a means to advance French power and leadership. One example was his sidelining of Euratom. Another was his veto which terminated in 1963 the first negotiations to enlarge the Community to include Britain, Denmark, Ireland, and Norway. Although the British government's conception of the Community was closer to that of de Gaulle than of the other, more federalist-minded member states' governments, and Britain's defence of its agricultural and Commonwealth interests had irked them by making the negotiations hard and long, they resented the unilateral and nationalist manner of the veto so deeply that it provoked the first political crisis within the Community. This was followed, in 1965, by a greater crisis over the arrangements for the common agricultural policy (CAP).

The CAP had from the outset been a key French interest and de Gaulle was determined to have it established without undue delay. It was to be based on price supports requiring substantial public expenditure. Both France and the Commission agreed that this should come from the budget of the Community, not the member states. But the Commission, with its federalist orientation, and the Dutch parliament, with its deep commitment to democratic principles, insisted that the budget spending must be subject to parliamentary control; and since a European budget could not be controlled by six separate parliaments, it would have to be done by the European Parliament. This suited the other governments well enough, but was anathema to de Gaulle. He precipitated the crisis of 'the empty chair', forbidding his ministers to attend meetings of the Council throughout the second half of 1965 and evoking fears among the other states that he might be preparing to destroy the Community.

Neither side was willing to give way and the episode concluded in January 1966 with the so-called 'Luxembourg compromise'. The French government asserted a right of veto when interests 'very important to one or more member states' are at stake; and the other five affirmed their commitment to the treaty provision for qualified majority voting on certain questions, which was that very month due to come into effect for votes on a wide range of subjects. It seems likely that the veto in the Council, rather than the role of the Parliament, was the crucial issue for de Gaulle; and though the other governments proclaimed their attachment to the principle of the majority vote, in practice de Gaulle's view prevailed for the next two decades, so that Luxembourg 'veto' seems a more accurate description than 'compromise'. In the mid-1980s, however, majority voting began to be practised in the context of the single market programme, and it has now become the standard procedure for most legislative decisions.

Despite these conflicts between the intergovernmental and the federal conceptions, the customs union was completed by July 1968, earlier than the treaty required. Its impact had already been felt not only internally but also in the Community's external relations. Wielding the common instrument of the external tariff, the Community was becoming, in the field of trade, a power comparable to the United States. President Kennedy had reacted by proposing multilateral negotiations for major tariff cuts. Skilfully led by the Commission, the Community responded positively; and the outcome was cuts averaging one-third, initiating an era in which it was to become the major force for international trade liberalization.

Alongside the ups and downs of Community politics, the Court of Justice made steady progress in establishing the rule of law. Based on its treaty obligation to ensure that 'the law is observed', in judgments in 1963 and 1964 the Court established the principles of the primacy and the direct effect of Community law, so that it would be consistently applied in all the member states. Though without the means of enforcement proper to a state, respect for the law, based on the treaties and on legislation enacted by its institutions, provided cement that has bound the Community together.

Widening and some deepening: Britain, Denmark, Ireland join

President de Gaulle resigned in 1969 and was replaced by Georges Pompidou. Nationalist fundamentalism as a basis for French policy gave way to pragmatic intergovernmentalism. Britain, Denmark, Ireland, and Norway still sought entry; France's partners supported it; and, instead of vetoing enlargement as de Gaulle had done, Pompidou consented, providing it was accompanied by conditions of interest to France, in particular agreement on the financing of the CAP, as well as elements of 'deepening' such as monetary union and coordination of foreign policy. In addition to serving the French agricultural interest, these were intended to further France's European project of integrating Germany yet more firmly into the Community, as well as guarding against the danger that widening the Community would weaken it.

France's partners favoured both widening and deepening. Germany's new Chancellor, the federalist Willy Brandt, played a leading part in a summit meeting of the six government heads in The Hague in December 1969. While he became famous for his Ostpolitik, relaxing tension with the Soviet bloc and with East Germany in particular, Brandt accompanied it with a Westpolitik for strengthening integration in the West. At The Hague he both promoted enlargement and proposed an economic and monetary union. This was agreed in principle, along with the other French conditions; and these projects were developed within the Community alongside the entry negotiations.

The principle of economic and monetary union was not, however, realized in practice until the 1990s. France, showing a preference for federal policy instruments rather than institutional reform, wanted a single currency. For Germany, this would have to be accompanied by coordination of economic policies, together with majority voting in the Council and powers for the European Parliament. But these were reforms too far for France in that early post-gaullist period. The result was a system for co-operation on exchange rates that was too weak to survive the international currency turbulence of that period. The system devised for foreign policy co-operation, kept separate from the Community owing to French insistence on sovereignty in this field, was strictly intergovernmental. Though quite useful, its impact was limited. It was the hard financial interest of French agriculture that secured a solid outcome, in a financial regulation that was to be highly disadvantageous for the British, whose small but efficient farm sector differed from those of the six member states.

The financing of the CAP again raised the question of powers for the European Parliament, on which the Dutch, supported by Belgium, Germany, and Italy, continued to insist. Pompidou's reaction was to accept the principle that the European Parliament would share control of the budget with the Council, but to exclude as much as possible of the expenditure, including in particular that on agriculture. This was accepted, faute de mieux, by France's partners in an amending treaty in 1970; and the Parliament's role was enhanced in a second treaty in 1975, after Pompidou had been succeeded by the post-gaullist President Giscard d'Estaing. While this was just a foot in the door to budgetary powers for the Parliament, it was to grow into a major element in the Community's institutional structure.

Though agriculture and Commonwealth trade still presented difficulties and the British public appeared unconvinced, Prime Minister Heath established good relations with President Pompidou and drove the entry negotiations through to a successful conclusion. Britain, together with Denmark and Ireland, joined the Community in January 1973, though the Norwegians rejected accession in a referendum. The British too were to vote in a referendum in 1975. Harold Wilson had replaced

6. British entry: Heath signs the Treaty of Accession.

Edward Heath as Prime Minister in 1974 following an election victory by the Labour Party, which was turning more and more against the Community. After a somewhat cosmetic 'renegotiation', the Wilson government did recommend continued membership; and in 1975 the voters approved it by a two-to-one majority. But Labour became increasingly hostile, to the point of campaigning in the 1983 elections for British withdrawal. Meanwhile Margaret Thatcher had become Prime Minister as a result of the Conservative election victory in 1979. While French post-gaullist governments were moving back towards support for earlier concepts of the Community, she was developing a stormy relationship with it, fighting to assert the principle of intergovernmentalism. Until 1984 she also fought to 'get our money back', as she put it, by blocking much Community business until she secured agreement to reduce Britain's high net contribution to the Community's budget.

European Council, direct elections, EMS

In 1974 President Pompidou died and Valéry Giscard d'Estaing succeeded him. Although Giscard had been de Gaulle's Finance Minister, he was not of the gaullist tradition and wanted to mark his presidency with measures to develop the Community. Ambivalent about federalism, he acted to strengthen both the intergovernmental and the federal elements in the Community's institutions, with initiatives to convert the summits into regular meetings, as the European Council of Heads of State and Government, as well as to launch direct elections to the European Parliament.

Following consultation with Monnet, who had remained active until then as President of the Action Committee for the United States of Europe in which he had brought together the leaders of the democratic political parties and trade unions of the member states, Giscard successfully proposed both the European Council and the direct elections. Although he seemed to envisage it would take the form of intimate chats among the heads of government, the European Council was soon to play a central part in taking Community decisions, settling conflicts that ministers in the Council were unable to resolve, and agreeing on major package deals. Provision had already been made for direct elections in the treaties of the 1950s, subject to a unanimous decision by the member states' governments. Unanimity had been unattainable while gaullists ruled France. But the governments now agreed and the first elections were held in June 1979. This step towards representative democracy was to have a big impact on the Community's future development.

That year of the first direct elections also saw a significant move towards monetary union. On becoming President of the Commission in 1977, Roy Jenkins, formerly a leading member of the Labour government, who without being explicitly federalist favoured steps in a federal direction, had looked for a way to 'move Europe forward' and concluded that the time was ripe to revive the idea of monetary union. This was taken up by the German Chancellor, Helmut Schmidt, who saw it as a way to spread the burden of a difficult relationship with the USA that resulted from the weakness of the dollar and the strength of the mark, and who was also influenced by Monnet's ideas. Schmidt and Giscard had forged a close relationship as Finance Ministers before becoming Chancellor and President in 1974; and they readily agreed on a proposal for a European Monetary System (EMS), with a strong mechanism for mutual exchange rate stability, and a European Currency Unit (ecu) to perform some technical functions. This was accepted by all save the British government, in the context of the Labour Party's growing hostility to the Community. So all but one of the member states participated in the EMS when it was created in 1979, alongside the Community rather than within it: an example of a recurrent pattern, with a number of states proceeding together while Britain, sometimes with one or two others, stands aside – usually deciding eventually to participate.

Single market, Draft Treaty on European Union, southern enlargement

Jacques Delors became President of the Commission in January 1985. He had visited each member state to find out what major project was likely to be accepted by all of them. As a federalist in Monnet's tradition, his shortlist contained projects – single market, single currency, institutional reform – that could be seen as steps in a federal direction. But Thatcher, whose view of federalism was akin to de Gaulle's, and so was hostile to the single currency and to institutional reform as Delors would conceive it, was at the same time a militant economic liberal who saw the single market as an important measure of trade liberalization. European economies had lost momentum during the hard times of the 1970s and all the governments accepted the single market project as a way to break out of what was then called eurosclerosis. The project was

7. Delors: single market, single currency, single-minded European.

strongly backed by the more dynamic firms and the main business associations.

The common market as conceived by the EEC Treaty was in effect a single internal market. But while the treaty had specified the programme for abolishing tariffs and quotas, which had thus been successfully accomplished, it had provided for unanimous voting in the Council on most of the legislation required to remove non-tariff barriers; and the effect of the Luxembourg 'compromise' had been to apply this veto under another name to the rest. The result was scant progress towards their removal, while a resurgence of protectionist pressures during the 1970s, combined with the increasing complexity of the modern economy, had made them a severe impediment to trade.

The successful abolition of tariffs on internal trade had demonstrated the value of a programme with a timetable. So the Commission produced a list of some 300 measures to be enacted by the end of 1992 in order to complete the single market by removing the non-tariff barriers. The Commissioner in charge of the project was Lord Cockfield, a former minister in the Thatcher government; and the programme was rapidly drafted in time to be presented to the European Council in Milan in June 1985.

Meanwhile the European Parliament had prepared a political project: a Draft Treaty on European Union, inspired by Altiero Spinelli, the leading figure among those federalists who saw the drafting of a constitution as the royal road to federation. He had pursued this idea since the 1950s and now saw the directly elected Members of the European Parliament (MEPs), of whom he was one, as qualified to draft it. He inspired fellow MEPs to support the project, led the process of drafting, and the Parliament approved the result by a big majority of votes.

The Draft Treaty was designed to reform the Community's institutions so as to give them a federal character; to extend its powers to include

8. Spinelli voting for his Draft Treaty on European Union.

most of those that would be normal in a federation, with the key exception of defence; and to come into effect when ratified by a majority of the member states containing at least two-thirds of the Community's population, with suitable arrangements to be negotiated with any states that did not ratify. While there was widespread support for the draft in most of the founder states, the German government was among those that were not prepared to countenance the probable exclusion of Britain. President Mitterrand did, however, express support for the draft, albeit in somewhat equivocal terms; and its main proposals were presented to the European Council in Milan along with the Commission's single market project.

The European Council decided to convene an Intergovernmental Conference (IGC) on treaty amendment, overriding British, Danish, and Greek opposition with its first-ever use of a majority vote. The IGC considered amendments relating not only to the single market programme but also to a number of the proposals in the Parliament's Draft Treaty. The outcome was the Single European Act, which provided for completion of the single market by 1992; gave the Community competences in the fields of the environment, technological research and development, social policies relating to employment, and 'cohesion'; and brought the foreign policy co-operation into the scope of the EEC Treaty – hence the title Single European Act, to distinguish it from a proposal to keep foreign policy separate. The Single Act also provided for qualified majority voting in a number of areas of single market legislation, and strengthened the European Parliament through a 'co-operation procedure' which gave it influence over such legislation, together with a procedure requiring its assent to treaties of association and accession.

The Community was enlarged in 1981 to include Greece and, in 1986, Portugal and Spain. All three had been ruled by authoritarian regimes and saw the Community as a support for their democracies as well as for economic modernization. The Community for its part wanted them to be viable member states and to be supportive of its projects, such as the single market. It was to this end that the cohesion policy, based on a doubling of the structural funds for assisting the development of economically weaker regions, was included in the Single Act.

Thus the Single Act strengthened both the Community's powers and its institutions, with influence from a combination of governments, economic interests, social concerns, the Commission, the Parliament, and a variety of federalist forces. It was succeeded by two further IGCs that led to the Maastricht and Amsterdam Treaties, likewise strengthening both powers and institutions, and responding to similar combinations of pressures. This would not have happened had the Single Act not been successful. But the prospect of the single market helped to revive the economy and the Community institutions gained in strength as they dealt with the vast programme of legislation.

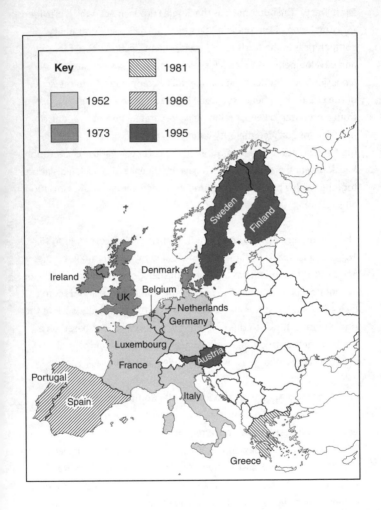

Key

1952	1981
1973	1986
1995	

Ireland

Denmark

Belgium

UK

Netherlands

Germany

Luxembourg

Austria

France

Portugal

Italy

Spain

Sweden

Finland

Greece

Map 1. Growth of the EU, 1952–2000.

Spinelli died a few weeks after the signing of the Single Act under the impression that it was a failure: 'a dead mouse', as he put it. In fact it initiated a relaunching of the Community which may have been as far-reaching in its effects as that which led to the Treaties of Rome.

Maastricht and Amsterdam Treaties

Following his success with the single market, Delors was determined to pursue the project of the single currency. Thatcher had not been alone in opposing it. Most Germans, proud of the deutschmark as the Community's strongest currency, were decidedly unenthusiastic. But it remained a major French objective, for economic as well as political reasons; and Kohl, a long-standing federalist, was persuaded that it would be a crucial step towards a federal Europe. While he facilitated the preparation of plans for the single currency, however, he faced difficulty in securing the necessary support in Germany.

The events of 1989 were a seismic upheaval. With the disintegration of the Soviet bloc, which opened up the prospect of enlarging the Community to the East, German unification also became possible. But Kohl needed Mitterrand's support: both for formal reasons because France, as an occupying power, had the right to veto German unification; and, pursuing the policy initiated by Brandt, to ensure that new eastern relationships did not undermine the European Community and the Franco-German partnership. Mitterrand saw the single currency as the way to anchor Germany irrevocably in the Community system, and hence as a condition for German unification; and this ensured for Kohl the necessary support in Germany to proceed with the project.

The result was the Maastricht Treaty, which provided not only for the euro and the European Central Bank but also for a number of other competences and institutional reforms. The Community was given some powers in the fields of education, youth, culture, and public health. Its institutions were strengthened in a number of

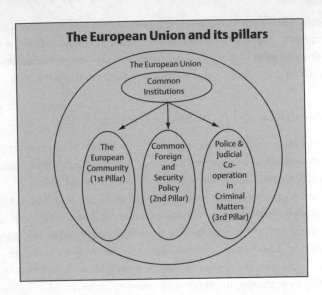

The European Union and its pillars

The European Union

Common Institutions

The European Community (1st Pillar)

Common Foreign and Security Policy (2nd Pillar)

Police & Judicial Co-operation in Criminal Matters (3rd Pillar)

ways, including more scope for qualified majority voting in the Council. The role of the European Parliament was enhanced through a 'co-decision' procedure that required its approval as well as that of the Council for laws in a number of fields; and it secured the right to approve – or not – the appointment of each new Commission. Two new 'pillars' were set up alongside the Community: one for a 'common foreign and security policy'; the other, relating to freedom of movement and internal security, for what was called 'co-operation in justice and home affairs' – renamed in the Amsterdam Treaty as 'police and judicial co-operation in criminal matters'. The basis for both was intergovernmental, though they were related to the Community institutions. The whole unwieldy structure was named the European Union, comprising the central, Community pillar as well as the other two.

Although John Major had succeeded Mrs Thatcher as Prime Minister with the avowed intention of moving to 'the heart of Europe', he insisted that Britain would participate neither in the single currency nor in a 'social chapter' on matters relating to employment. In order to secure agreement on the treaty as a whole, it was accepted that Britain could opt out of both, together with Denmark as far as the single currency was concerned.

The Maastricht Treaty was signed in February 1992 and entered into force in November 1993 after a number of vicissitudes: two Danish referenda, in the first of which it was rejected and in the second approved after some small adjustments had been made; a French referendum in which the voters accepted it by a tiny majority; in London, a fraught ratification process in the House of Commons; and in Germany a lengthy deliberation by the Constitutional Court before it rejected a claim that the treaty was unconstitutional. These episodes, together with evidence that citizens' approval of the Union was declining in most member states, seemed alarming, particularly to people of federalist orientation.

The more federalist among the governments, however, felt that the Maastricht Treaty did not go far enough. With the decisive new monetary powers and the prospect of further enlargement, first to some of the few remaining West European states that were not already members, then to many more from Central and Eastern Europe, these wanted to make the Union more effective and democratic. So the treaty provided for another IGC; and the result was the Amsterdam Treaty, signed in 1997 and in force in 1999.

The Amsterdam Treaty revisited a number of the Union's competences, including those relating to the two intergovernmental pillars. A new chapter on employment was added to the Community Treaty, reflecting concern about the unemployment that had persisted through the 1990s at a level around 10 per cent, together with fears that it might be aggravated if the European Central Bank were to pursue a tight money policy.

Among the institutions, the European Parliament gained most, with co-decision extended to include the majority of legislative decisions, and the right of approval over the appointment not only of the Commission as a whole, but before that, of its President. Since the President, once approved, was given the right to accept or reject the nominations for the other members of the Commission, the Parliament's power over the Commission was considerably enhanced. Its part in the process that led to the Commission's resignation in March 1999 and in the appointment of the new Commission demonstrated the significance of parliamentary control over the executive. The treaty also gave the Commission's President more power over the other Commissioners.

At the same time as adding these federal elements to the institutions, the Amsterdam Treaty reflected fears that the Union would not be able to meet the challenges ahead if new developments were to be inhibited by the unanimity procedure. This led to a procedure of 'enhanced co-operation', allowing a group of member states to proceed with a project in which a minority did not wish to participate: generalizing, in fact, the cases of the single currency and the social chapter. Six weeks before the meeting of the European Council in Amsterdam that reached agreement on the treaty, however, Tony Blair became Prime Minister following Labour's election victory. The new British government adopted the social chapter and, expressing a more favourable attitude towards the Union, accepted without demur such reforms as the increase in the Parliament's powers. But Britain, along with Denmark and Ireland, did opt out of the provision to abolish frontier controls, along with the partial transfer of the related co-operation in justice and home affairs to the Community pillar, even if the British government was later to co-operate quite energetically in that field. As regards external security, Europe's weak performance in former Yugoslavia had spurred demands for a stronger defence capacity; and Britain both accepted provision for this in the Amsterdam Treaty and then joined with France to initiate action along these lines.

Enlargement to the North and the East; the IGC 2000

Austria, Finland, and Sweden joined the Union in January 1995. The Norwegian government too had negotiated an accession treaty but it was again rejected in a referendum. This time the Swiss government also applied, but withdrew its application in 1992 after defeat in a referendum on participation in the European Economic Area, which is a much looser form of relationship with the Union.

This round of enlargement was accompanied by virtually no specific measures of deepening. No economic problems were raised by these prosperous market economies. The growing number of member states, not all of them expected to favour further strengthening of the institutions, did however contribute to pressure from the more federalist states for institutional reform in the Treaty of Amsterdam, which was reinforced by the prospect of the further enlargement to come.

Following their emergence from Soviet domination, ten Central and East European states obtained association with the Union, and then sought accession. They faced an enormous task of transforming their economies and polities from centralized communist control to the market economies and pluralist democracies that membership required. But by 1997 the Union judged that five of them had made enough progress to justify starting accession negotiations in the following year; and negotiations with another five opened in January 2000. The countries in the first wave were the Czech Republic, Estonia, Hungary, Poland, and Slovenia, together with Cyprus whose application was also on the table. The second wave included Bulgaria, Latvia, Lithuania, Romania, and Slovakia, together with Malta. Turkey's candidature was also recognized; but the economic and political problems were such that no date was fixed for starting negotiations.

With such a formidable enlargement ahead, the question of deepening arose again. Reform of some policies was necessary, in particular for agriculture and the structural funds. The Commission's proposals for this, entitled *Agenda 2000*, were partially adopted, though it is likely that further measures will be required. As regards reform of the institutions, another IGC was convened in 2000. There were two views as to what it should do: one, that it should stick to a minimal agenda, on the number of Commissioners, the weighting of votes in the Council to avoid domination by the large number of smaller states that were likely to join in the coming years, and an extension of the scope of qualified majority voting; the other, that a more radical reform was required. As we shall see, the Treaty of Nice, agreed when the European Council concluded the IGC in December 2000 and likely to enter into force in 2002 at latest, came closer to a minimal than to a radical reform.

Chapter 3
How the EU is governed

The EU has major economic and environmental powers, and is increasingly active in foreign policy, defence, and internal security. How is this power used and controlled? How is the Union governed?

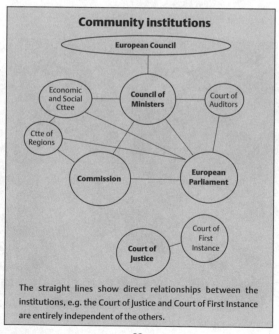

Community institutions

European Council

Economic and Social Cttee

Council of Ministers

Court of Auditors

Ctte of Regions

Commission

European Parliament

Court of First Instance

Court of Justice

The straight lines show direct relationships between the institutions, e.g. the Court of Justice and Court of First Instance are entirely independent of the others.

The answer, according to many intergovernmentalists, is through co-operation among the governments of member states: the other institutions are peripheral to the Council in which the governments are represented, and this fact will not go away. But while the Council is still the most powerful institution, federalists regard the Parliament, Commission, and Court of Justice not only as sufficiently independent of the states to have changed the nature of the relationships among them, but also as major actors in a process that may, and should, result in the Union becoming a federal polity.

The European Council and the Council

The Council consists of ministers representing the member states; and at the highest level there is the European Council of Heads of State or

9. European Council, 1979: facing different ways.

Government together with the President of the European Commission. Heads of state are included in the title because the Presidents of France and Finland participate as well as their prime ministers, since they have some of the functions performed by heads of government elsewhere.

The European Council meets three or four times a year and takes decisions that require resolution or impulsion at that political level, sometimes because ministers have been unable to resolve an issue in the Council, sometimes because a package deal involving many subjects, such as the Maastricht or Amsterdam Treaty, has to be assembled. The European Council also has to 'define general political guidelines'. Its rotating presidency is an important function, both for the efficient management of current business and for launching new projects.

The meetings themselves are quite small, with the three presidents (of France, Finland, and the Commission) and fifteen heads of government accompanied by foreign ministers, and sometimes finance ministers. But they are surrounded by a vast media circus which presents the results to the citizens of different countries in radically different ways. Thus readers of British newspapers could have been forgiven for supposing that the European Council in Helsinki in December 1999 was dominated by quarrels between Britain and France about beef and between Britain and the rest about proposals for a tax affecting the financial interests of the City of London. Yet beef was not on the agenda and tax took up only a little time. Many journalists in other countries emphasized the decisions to open entry negotiations with six more states and to establish a rapid reaction force to help with peace-keeping.

The 'Presidency Conclusions' are issued after each meeting, usually in a lengthy document, sometimes with bulky annexes. Of course the heads of state and government themselves initiate only a few of their decisions, and do not have time or inclination for thorough discussion of all that is put before them. They do initiate some major projects, as for example the rapid reaction force, which was a joint British and French proposal. But most of the detail and of the 'political guidelines' emerge from the Union's institutions, working with the European Council's President-in-Office.

The Council of Ministers is a more complicated body. Which minister attends a given meeting depends on the subject. It meets in over a score of forms, ranging from an Economic and Financial Council (Ecofin), an Agriculture Council, and a Justice and Home Affairs Council, to Councils for Health, for Tourism, and for Youth. There is also a General Affairs Council comprising the foreign ministers, which is supposed to coordinate the work of the other Councils, but is in practice hard put to it to control Councils of ministers from powerful departments of state. The incoherence of this structure has been recognized by the European Council, which decided in 1999 that the number of Councils should

10. Council of Ministers: not a cosy conclave.

be reduced to not more than fifteen: not exactly a radical reform. Each Council is, like the European Council, chaired by the representative of the state that is serving in turn for six months as President-in-Office.

Unlike the European Council, large numbers attend the meetings of the Council. Several officials as well as the ministers from each member state are present; and they are joined by the relevant Commissioners. Officials from the Commission also attend, as well as those from the Council Secretariat, which provides continuity from one presidency to the next and has become quite a powerful institution. Also unlike the European Council, much of the Council's work is legislative and some is executive.

The Council's proceedings are more like negotiations in a diplomatic conference than a debate in a normal democratic legislature. Most of its legislative sessions are not open to the public. They are far from secret; but the information that gets out comes mainly from what the various ministers tell the media after the meetings: sometimes in sharply divergent accounts.

The resemblance to an international negotiation was yet more pronounced before the mid-1980s when, with the launching of the single market programme, qualified majority voting (QMV) began to replace unanimity as the procedure for legislative decisions. Though the treaty stipulated that only texts proposed by the Commission could be enacted into law, the unanimity procedure had given each minister a veto with which to pressure the Commission into amending its proposal as he (yes, then almost always he) required; and although the treaty provided for QMV on a range of subjects, the veto implicit in the Luxembourg 'compromise' extended its scope in practice to virtually the whole of legislation. The Committee of Permanent Representatives of the member states (called Coreper, after its French acronym) seeks common ground beforehand in the governments' reactions to the

Commission's proposals; and given the difficulty of securing unanimity, it was thanks to the dedication of many of these officials that the Community was able to function at all. But measures identified by the Commission as being in the general interest and enjoying the support of a large majority were often reduced to a 'lowest common denominator', reached after long delay.

This contributed to the failure to make much progress towards the single market until the voting procedures were changed following the Single European Act. Up to then, single market measures had been passed at a rate of about one a month, barely enough to keep up with new developments in the economy, let alone complete the whole programme inside a quarter of a century. But the Single Act's provision for QMV on most of the single market legislation helped speed the rate to about one a week, putting the bulk of the laws in place by 1992.

The qualified majority among the fifteen member states is sixty-two out of the total of eighty-seven weighted votes. The weights depend on size: France, Germany, Italy, and the UK have ten votes each, Luxembourg two, the others in between. Since a decision can be blocked by twenty-six votes, laws cannot be passed against the wishes of any three of the largest states. The forthcoming accession of a dozen or more new states, mostly quite small, caused the large ones to fear that the balance will tilt against them. So the Nice Treaty sets new weights, as from 1 January 2005, ranging from twenty-nine each for the four largest states to four for Luxembourg. With the qualified majority of just over 70 per cent of the 237 votes, any three of the largest could still block a decision; and as enlargement proceeds, this will remain the case, save that Britain, France, and Italy combined will come to need the support of at least a small one. Germany, with the biggest population, has the additional edge that the qualified majority will have to contain at least 62 per cent of the Union's population, while to protect the smaller ones, at least a simple majority of states will be required.

While QMV is designed to ensure that laws wanted by a substantial majority can be passed, the Council still tries to avoid overriding a minority of one government about something it regards as important. This is due partly to the need to treat minorities with care in a diverse polity, as is the case in the Swiss federal system; and that motive has an edge in the EU, where a disgruntled government could retaliate by bringing business to a halt on other matters still subject to unanimity. Partly it reflects the diplomatic culture which prevails in the Council. But the difference between that and the 'Luxembourg veto' is that a vote is in fact quite often taken; and proceedings take place in what has been called 'the shadow of the vote', so that ministers prefer to compromise than to run the risk that a vote will produce an outcome which is worse for them. Often the President, judging that a problem has been resolved, suggests that a consensus has been reached and, if there is no dissent, the Council accepts the text without a formal vote.

With the use of QMV for single market legislation, the Luxembourg veto began to fade away, so that QMV became the context for a wider range of decisions; and it was extended by the Maastricht, Amsterdam and Nice Treaties to cover some four-fifths of all legislative acts. The remaining one-fifth or so of acts to which unanimity applied come under a variety of headings. Britain was among those that insisted it apply to some aspects of employment-related social policy, for reasons of ideology as well as subsidiarity. Money, rather than ideology, was the motive of those who opposed QMV for decisions on the aims, tasks, and organization of the structural funds. There is British insistence on unanimity for tax harmonization, partly on grounds of sovereignty. Treaty amendments raising the ceiling for the Union's tax revenue and treaties of accession or even association have been held to touch sovereignty so closely that they must be ratified by each member state. While the Nice Treaty provides QMV for nomination of the President and other members of the Commission, and the Secretary-General of the Council, the states have kept their veto over other major appointments such as Judges of the Court of Justice and Executive Board members of the European Central Bank, which have to be made by 'common accord' among the governments. Unanimity also prevails in the other two pillars, as Chapters 7 and 8 show.

The greater the number of member states, the harder it becomes to reach unanimous agreement. So with the prospect of enlargement, pressure has grown to reduce the scope for the unanimity procedure, as the Nice Treaty indeed does, if not to eliminate it altogether; and this is a source of conflict between those with more, or less, federalist orientation. A similar argument arises about the Council's executive role.

Unlike a legislative body in most democracies, the Council exercises significant executive powers. Although the Commission is, as Monnet envisaged, the Community's principal executive body, the Treaty allows the Council to 'impose requirements' on the way in which the Commission implements the laws, or even to see to their implementation itself. The Council disposes of a large number of committees of member states' officials to supervise the Commission's implementation and of 'working parties' to examine its legislative proposals, the whole network being controlled by Coreper. Each committee specializes in a branch of Community activity. They can be a useful means of liaison between the Commission and the states' administrations, to which the bulk of the execution of Community policies is in fact delegated. But the procedure that the Council has laid down for some of the committees makes it possible for officials from a minority of states to block the Commission's action until such time as the matter comes before the Council, which may then confirm the decision to block. This has led to complaints that the 'comitology', as the system is ironically called, undermines the Community's efficiency; and the European Parliament, where it has the right to co-decide legislation, has used this to minimize the committees' blocking power. A committee may well be justified in resisting something the Commission wants to do in a particular case. But in general, it seems hardly credible that such a vast and complex matter as the execution of a wide range of the Community's policies could in effect be the responsibility of a body comprising the representatives of fifteen or more separate governments.

The European Parliament

Members of the European Parliament (MEPs) are directly elected by citizens throughout the Union in June of every fifth year. There are 626 of them, distributed among the member states in proportions that favour the smaller states, though to a lesser degree than in the weighting of votes in the Council: ranging from ninety-nine from Germany, eighty-seven each from France, Italy, and the UK, down to fifteen from the Irish Republic and six from Luxembourg. Here again, the Nice Treaty has provided for the forthcoming enlargement by a new distribution among the states, within a total not to exceed 732 seats, to apply as from the elections of June 2004.

The political culture of the European Parliament differs radically from

Number of MEPs from each state

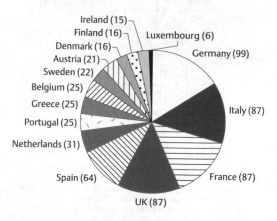

Total number of MEPs 626

41

that of the Council. The meetings are open to the public; voting by simple majority is the routine; and the MEPs usually vote by party group rather than by state. Three-quarters of the MEPs elected in June 1999 belonged to the mainstream party groups: 233 to the centre-right Christian Democrat and Conservative EPP (European People's Party) Group; 180 to the centre-left PES (Party of European Socialists) Group; and 51 to the ELDR (European Liberals, Democrats and Reformists) Group. The rest were evenly divided between smaller groups to the left, of which the most important were the Greens, and to the right with a variety of eurosceptics – including a French party called 'Hunters and Fishermen', opposing EU legislation that affects those sports.

While agreement has not yet been reached on a uniform electoral

Party groups in the Parliament after the 1999 elections

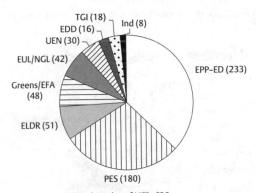

TGI (18)
EDD (16)
UEN (30)
EUL/NGL (42)
Greens/EFA (48)
ELDR (51)
Ind (8)
EPP–ED (233)
PES (180)

Total number of MEPs 626

EPP–ED:	Group of the European People's Party and European Democrats
PES:	Group of the Party of European Socialists
ELDR:	Group of the European Liberal, Democratic and Reformist Party
Greens/EFA:	Group of the Greens/European Free Alliance
EUL/NGL:	Confederal Group of the European United Left/Nordic Green Left
UEN:	Group of the Union for a Europe of Nations
EDD:	Europe of Democracies and Diversities Group
TGI:	Technical Group of Independent Members
Ind:	Independent

procedure, or 'principles common to all member states' as the Amsterdam Treaty more tolerantly put it, all the states now operate systems of proportional representation: ten with national lists, four (Belgium, Ireland, Italy, UK) with a regional basis, and one (Germany) with both. The swings in the balance between parties have hitherto been caused mainly by Britain's first-past-the-post system, whose effect was to reduce the number of Conservative MEPs from sixty in 1979 to seventeen in 1994, while that of Labour rose from seventeen to sixty-two. But the proportional representation introduced for the 1999 elections moderated the swing, returning thirty-six Conservatives and twenty-nine Labour – together with ten Liberal Democrats, compared with only two in 1994 from a larger share of the vote.

As proportional representation has been used in all the other states, the balance between the mainstream parties has been fairly stable, with neither the centre-right nor the centre-left able to command a majority. So a broad coalition across the centre is needed to ensure a majority for voting on legislation or the budget; and this is all the more necessary for amending or rejecting measures under the increasingly important co-decision procedure, where an absolute majority of 314 votes is required. The well-developed system of committees, each preparing the Parliament's positions and grilling the Commissioners in a field of the Union's activities, also tends to encourage consensual behaviour. But there has none the less been a sharper left – right division since the elections of 1999.

Although the Parliament has performed well enough in using its now considerable powers over legislation and the budget, the voters' turnout has declined with each election, from 63.0 per cent in 1979 to 49.4 per cent in 1999. One reason is a general trend of declining turnouts in elections within member states. Another is a widespread decline in support for the Union during the 1990s. Yet another may be that the Parliament in particular has been exposed to critical and, particularly in Britain, downright hostile media comment, fastening on matters such as the failure (largely the fault of MEPs themselves) to establish an adequate system for controlling their expenses, and the two costly buildings in Brussels and Strasbourg between which it commutes (this being the fault of member state governments). Citizens may, moreover, not yet be aware how much the Parliament's powers have grown, following the Maastricht and Amsterdam Treaties.

The legislative role has developed from mere consultation at first, through the co-operation procedure initiated by the Single Act, to the co-decision introduced by the Maastricht Treaty and extended at Amsterdam to the point where it now applies to over half the legislation. Already in 1989 the Parliament could use its influence under the co-operation procedure to secure results such as stricter standards for exhaust emissions from small cars. With co-decision it has been able, among other things, to limit the Council's tendency to extend control of its committees of national officials over the Commission's execution of

11. Elected representatives at work: European Parliament sitting.

Community policies. It has used its power of assent over association agreements as a sanction against human rights abuse in Turkey, and to ensure better conditions for Palestinians exporting to the Community from the occupied territories.

In a typical example of Union jargon that is hard for the public to understand, the budgetary expenditure is divided into CE (compulsory expenditure) and NCE (non-compulsory expenditure). The CE was opaquely defined as 'expenditure necessarily resulting from this Treaty or from acts adopted in accordance therewith'. It was in fact designed to avoid parliamentary control over the agricultural expenditure, which France saw as a major national interest; and the Parliament has indeed fought to limit the growth of that part of the budget. But while its power over the CE is limited, the Parliament has the edge over the Council for the NCE which, along with the expansion of the structural funds, has grown until it now accounts for over half the total expenditure. One example of the Parliament's use of its powers was the increase in the aid for economic transformation in Central and East European countries after they emerged from Soviet control.

While the Parliament's share of power to determine the budget is an essential element of democratic control, its role in supervising how the money is spent has had the greatest impact. As well as its power of scrutiny over the Commission's administrative and financial activities, the Parliament has the right to grant 'discharge': to approve – or not – the Commission's implementation of the previous year's budget, on the basis of a report from the Court of Auditors. Normally, if not satisfied, the Parliament withholds discharge until the Commission has undertaken to do what is required. Thus in 1992 it delayed the grant of discharge for the 1990 accounts until the Commission had agreed to allocate fifty members of its staff to an anti-fraud unit. But in 1998, after the Parliament had withheld discharge for the 1996 accounts and was not satisfied with the Commission's response, it appointed a high-level

45

expert committee to investigate in more detail. They produced a devastating report on mismanagement and some cases of corruption; and the Commission, anticipating the Parliament's use of its power of dismissal, resigned in March 1999.

The Parliament then used the powers it had gained in the Maastricht and Amsterdam Treaties over the appointment of the new Commission. First it made full use of its power over the appointment of the Commission's President, interviewing Romano Prodi to make sure he was not only a suitable choice for President but would also pursue the reforms and policy orientations that MEPs wanted, before approving his nomination by the governments. Then it did the same with each of the other Commissioners before approving the appointment of the Commission as a whole. Prodi and most of the Commissioners accepted the mainstream view among MEPs; and the result was a successful start to the relationship between the new Commission and the new Parliament.

The Parliament shares power equally with the Council for only some half of the legislation and the budget. But it has proved much better able than the Council to control the Commission. So it may be said that the Parliament is more than halfway towards fulfilling the functions of enacting legislation and controlling the executive, which a house of the citizens in a federal legislature would perform. The Council for its part would be akin to a house of the states, save that the unanimity procedure still applies to one-fifth of the legislation, its legislative sessions are not held in public, and it has retained executive powers that ill accord with its legislative role.

The Economic and Social Committee and the Committee of the Regions

Alongside the Parliament and the Council, the Community has two advisory bodies: the Economic and Social Committee (Ecosoc) and the

Representation by state in Economic and Social Committee and Committee of the Regions

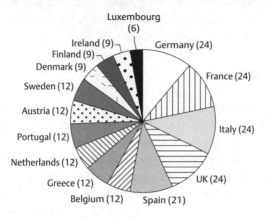

Total in each Committee 222 members

Committee of the Regions. The Commission and Council must consult them on certain subjects specified by the treaty; the Commission, Council or Parliament may consult them on any subject; and they can issue their 'opinions' on their own initiative. Both have 222 members, nominated by the states and appointed by the Council. The Nice Treaty provides for the number to rise to a maximum of 344 as enlargement proceeds to a total of twenty-seven states.

The members of Ecosoc represent a wide range of economic and social interests. Those of the Committee of the Regions are representatives of regional and local bodies. Both produce reports that are useful, though not usually influential. But with the influence that the German Länder already exert in Community affairs, and the growing strength of regional representation in other member states, of which the Scottish Parliament and Welsh Assembly are notable examples, the Committee of the Regions may well gain more influence in future.

The European Commission

While the Commission, as it stands today, is not the federal executive that Monnet envisaged, it is, with its right of 'legislative initiative' and its functions in executing Community policies and as 'watchdog of the Treaty', a great deal more than the secretariat of an international organization.

The Treaty of Rome gives the Commission the sole right of legislative initiative, that is, to propose the texts for laws to the Parliament and the Council. The aim was to ensure that the laws would be based more on a view of the general interest of the Community and its citizens than could result from initiatives of the member state governments, and that there would be more coherence in the legislative programme than they or the Councils with their various functional responsibilities could provide. Armed with this power, the Commission was in its early days often called the 'motor of the Community'. After it had been weakened by de Gaulle's assault in the 1960s, the balance of power swung towards the Council and, since its establishment in 1974, the European Council. But the Commission still performs the essential role of initiating both particular measures for the Council and Parliament to decide, and general policy packages that the President-in-Office steers through the European Council. Outstanding examples of the latter were the 'Delors package' of budgetary reform that the European Council adopted in 1992 under British presidency, and the *Agenda 2000* reforms of Community policies to prepare for the Eastern enlargement that were agreed under German presidency in 1999. Thus the Commission can still be a motor for the Union's development.

The Commission has also been called the 'watchdog' because it has to ensure that the Community's treaty and laws are applied, notably by the member states. If it has evidence of an infringement, it has to issue a 'reasoned opinion' to the state in question. Should the latter fail to comply, the Commission can take it to the Court of Justice. This is what happened in 1999 when the French government refused to accept the Community's decision that British beef was by then safe to eat and its import should be allowed. Because of its backlog of work, the Court may take up to two years to issue its judgment. But if France is then found to be in the wrong, the Court can impose an appropriate fine. The Commission is also responsible for executing Community law and policy, though much of it is delegated to member state governments and other agencies.

In order to ensure that the Commission works in the general interest of the Community, the treaty requires that its independence of any outside interests be 'beyond doubt'; and the Commissioners, on taking up office, have to make a 'solemn undertaking' to that effect. There are at present twenty of them, two each from France, Italy, Germany, Spain, and the UK, and one each from the smaller states. Although the treaty provides for their nomination by 'common accord' among the governments, each government has in the past made its own nomination and this has been accepted by the others. But the accord of the Commission's newly appointed President is now also required before the Parliament's approval of the Commission as a whole. So the choice is subject to new influences.

As with the Council and Parliament, the impending enlargement causes concern that a larger Commission would be less effective. So the Nice Treaty limits the number of Commissioners, as from 2005, to one from each member state. Proposals for a smaller number were stoutly resisted by smaller states such as Ireland. Their argument is that, although Commissioners are appointed not to represent their countries but to serve the general interest, this will not be served unless they have enough knowledge of the conditions and political cultures of the different states. There may be a fine line between bringing that knowledge to bear and promoting the national interest; but a change in the number of Commissioners requires unanimous agreement on a treaty amendment, so agreement was reached only on what is to happen in a fairly distant future when the twenty-seventh state joins the Union; and the Treaty provides that a decision is to be taken then to limit the number of Commissioners to fewer than twenty-seven.

Reducing the number of Commissioners to fewer than one per state is not the only way to secure effectiveness. The top tier of governments, such as the British Cabinet, usually has over twenty members, in some cases over thirty; and this has worked because a Prime Minister has the power to control the other members. The Amsterdam Treaty moved the Commission some way in that direction by giving the President the rights to share in the decisions to nominate the other Commissioners and to exercise 'political guidance' over the Commissioners, together with the opportunity to allocate and 'reshuffle' their responsibilities; and the Nice Treaty gives the President the power not only to allocate and reshuffle responsibilities but also to appoint Vice-Presidents, and to sack a Commissioner 'after obtaining the collective approval of the Commission'.

12. First meeting of the new Commission, 1999: President Prodi enjoys a laugh.

In treaty terminology, the Commission is the twenty Commissioners. In common usage, it also refers to the Commission's staff. But it is usually clear whether reference is being made to the twenty Commissioners or the sixteen thousand officials; and despite loose talk of a bloated bureaucracy, this is fewer than the numbers employed by many local authorities.

Since QMV now applies to the bulk of legislation, the Commission's sole right of initiative has given it a strong position in the legislative process. The Council can amend the Commission's text, but only by unanimity, which here works in the Commission's favour instead of against it. While the Commission normally prefers to accommodate governments' wishes, it is better placed to resist their pressure on points it regards as important.

The Commission has performed its legislative role well. But its performance as an executive has been heavily criticized. Much of the criticism has been unfair, where the execution is in fact delegated to the member states. This is a good principle, which works well in Germany's federal system where the Länder administer most of the federal policies. But there the federal government has the power to ensure adequate performance from the Länder, whereas member states tend to resist the Commission's efforts to supervise them. The answer is surely not more direct administration by Brussels, but enough Commission staff to undertake the supervision and stronger powers to ensure proper implementation by the states.

The Commission has a good record in fields such as the administration of competition policy, where it was given the power to do the job itself and has done it well despite a shortage of officials. But there have been serious defects where it has been required to administer expenditure programmes without the staff who can do it properly, with the consequence either of defects in its own work or in that of consultants hired to do it, with sometimes bad and in a few cases fraudulent results.

Such defects, as well as those due to inadequate administrative practices and sense of financial responsibility, were among the criticisms of the report that led to the Commission's resignation in 1999 and to insistence that the new Commission must carry out radical administrative reform.

Romano Prodi and Neil Kinnock, the Vice-President of the Commission responsible for its reform, confront a system which has changed little during the four decades of its existence, and which has been subject to pressure from governments insisting on specific senior appointments for their own nationals and from staff unions resistant to change. The reforms that Prodi and Kinnock propose include changes in recruitment, training, promotion, and disciplinary procedures; a new audit unit in the Commission to ensure funds are spent properly; and an 'inter-institutional committee' to oversee standards of behaviour in the Commission, the Council, and the Parliament.

Prodi has been bold enough to suggest that the Commission is a European government. How far is this an accurate description? Within the fields of Community competence, its right of legislative initiative resembles that of a government, and even exceeds it in so far as the Commission's is a sole right. But its use of the right is constrained by the Council, particularly where the unanimity procedure applies, though also by the use of QMV rather than a simple majority. The difference is, however, greater in comparison with Britain than with states that practise a consensual style of coalition government. The Commission's executive role is constrained by the Council and the comitology but is otherwise not, in principle, far different from that of the German federal government, though in practice the German government has more effective means to enforce proper implementation by the Länder. A crucial distinction between the Commission and a government is, indeed, that the former does not control any physical means of enforcement. It has moreover only a minor role in general foreign policy, and virtually none in defence. Along with the differences, however, there are significant similarities.

The Court of Justice

The rule of law has been a key to the success of the European Community. Increasingly, in its fields of competence, a framework of law rather than relative power governs the relations between member states and applies to their citizens. This establishes 'legal certainty', which is prized by business people because it reduces a major element of risk in their transactions. Politically, it has helped to create the altogether new climate in which war between the states is held to be unthinkable.

At the apex of the Community's legal system is the Court of Justice, which the treaty requires to ensure that 'the law', comprising the treaty itself and legislation duly enacted by the institutions, 'is observed'.

13. Rule of law: the Court of Justice sitting.

There is one judge from each member state, appointed for six-year terms by common accord among the member states and whose independence is to be 'beyond doubt'. The Court itself judges cases such as those concerning the legality of Community acts, or actions by the Commission against a member state or by one member state against another, alleging failure to fulfil a treaty obligation. But the vast majority of cases involving Community law are those brought by individuals or companies against other such legal persons or governments; and these are tried in the member states' courts, coming before the Court of Justice only if one of those courts asks it to interpret a point of law.

The Court's most fundamental judgments, delivered in the 1960s, were based on its determination to ensure that the law was observed as the treaty required. The first, on the primacy of Community law, was designed to ensure its even application in all the member states; for the rule of law would progressively disintegrate should it be overridden by divergent national laws. The second, on direct effect, provided for individuals to claim their rights under the treaty directly in the states' courts. Then in 1979 a judgment on the 'Cassis de Dijon' case laid a cornerstone of the single market programme, with the principle of 'mutual recognition' of member states' standards for the safety of products, provided they were judged acceptable; and this radically reduced the need for detailed regulation at the Community level. In 1985 the Court required the Council to fulfil its treaty obligation, outstanding since 1968, to adopt a common transport policy; and the Council duly complied.

The Court has by now delivered some 5,000 judgments and cases continue to come before it at a rate that makes it hard to reduce the delays of up to two years before judgments are reached. A 'Court of First Instance' was established to help deal with this problem, hearing almost all cases brought by individuals or legal persons, which relate mainly to competition policy and to disputes between Community institutions and their staff. But this has stemmed, not turned, the tide of cases awaiting judgment.

While litigants can appeal from the Court of First Instance to the Court of Justice on points of law (hence the words 'first instance'), there is no appeal beyond the Court of Justice, which is the final judicial authority on matters within Community competence. To enforce its judgments, however, it depends on the enforcement agencies of the member states. The fact that the large majority of judgments under Community law are made by the states' own courts has instilled the habit of enforcing it; and there has been no refusal to enforce the judgments of the Court itself, even if there have sometimes been quite long delays before member states have complied with judgments that went against them.

The Court's jurisdiction is almost entirely confined to the fields of Community competence and, to some extent, the 'pillar' dealing with police and judicial co-operation. But within these limits, and apart from the almost total reliance on the member states' enforcement agencies, the Community's legal system has largely federal characteristics.

Subsidiarity and flexibility

In a speech delivered in Bruges in 1988, Mrs Thatcher famously evoked the spectre of a 'European super-state exercising a new dominance from Brussels'; and a 'slippery slope' leading towards a 'centralized super-state' has become a favourite metaphor for British eurosceptics. From a different starting-point, German Länder have looked askance at proposals for Union competence in fields that belong to them in Germany's federal system. Indeed many federalists find the treaty objective of 'an ever closer union' too open-ended, and most support the principle of 'subsidiarity' as a guide to determine what the Union should do and what it should not do. That principle, which has both

Calvinist and Catholic antecedents, requires bodies with responsibilities for larger areas to perform only the functions that those responsible for smaller areas within them cannot do for themselves. Following this principle, the treaty requires the Community to 'take action . . . only if and insofar as the objective of the proposed action cannot be sufficiently achieved by the Member States', and can, 'by reason of its scale or effects, be better achieved by the Community'.

The Rome Treaty implicitly recognized this principle in distinguishing between two kinds of Community act: the Regulation, which is 'binding in its entirety' on all the member states; and the Directive, which is binding only 'as to the result to be achieved', leaving each state to choose the 'form and methods'. But this was a very partial application of the principle; and Directives were sometimes enacted in such detail as to leave little choice to the states. So the Maastricht Treaty defined subsidiarity and the Amsterdam Treaty laid down detailed procedures aiming to ensure that the principle would be practised by the Community institutions. Some federalists, finding this an insufficient safeguard against over-centralization, have proposed that the treaty should list competences reserved to member states. As a result of German pressure in particular, the European Council agreed at Nice that a further IGC be convened in 2004, among other things to clarify the division of powers between the Union and the states.

There are of course disagreements about the fields in which integration is justified. These left their mark on the Maastricht Treaty, in the British opt-outs from the social chapter and the single currency, and those of Denmark on the single currency and defence. Since the treaty can be amended only by unanimity, the other governments had to accept the opting-out if these items were to be included in it; and this led to growing interest in the idea of 'flexibility', enabling those states wanting further integration in a given field to proceed within the Community institutions or, to put it the other way round, letting a minority opt out. One purpose was to circumvent the veto of the UK or

Denmark, where there was strong resistance to further integration. Although British policy changed after Labour's election victory in 1997, there are still fears that there will be British and Scandinavian opposition to reforms which most other governments regard as necessary in order to prepare for the Eastern enlargement; and it is also feared that some of the new member states may then prove unwilling or unable to proceed with further integration, or even to cope effectively with integration as it stands.

The concept of flexibility emerged in the Amsterdam Treaty under the heading of 'enhanced co-operation', a term preferred by federalists because it implied a deeper level of integration among a group of states, whereas eurosceptics tended to see flexibility as a way of loosening bonds in the Community as a whole. The Amsterdam Treaty provided for enhanced co-operation within the Community provided that a number of conditions were met, including unanimous agreement that it be applied in any given case; but the Nice Treaty allows any group of eight or more states to proceed if a qualified majority agree.

Citizens

The concept of citizenship of the Union was introduced in the Maastricht Treaty, which provided that all nationals of the member states are also citizens of the Union; and the Amsterdam Treaty added that the two forms of citizenship are complementary. The Maastricht Treaty included a few new rights for the citizens, such as to move and reside freely throughout the Union subject to specified conditions, and to vote or stand in other member states in local and European, though not national, elections. This short list comes on top of specific rights already guaranteed by the treaties, such as protection for member states' citizens against discrimination based on nationality in fields of Community competence, and equal treatment for men and women in matters relating to employment. The Union's institutions are also required to respect fundamental rights, as guaranteed by the European Convention on Human Rights and Fundamental Freedoms.

Until the Amsterdam Treaty, there was no treaty provision requiring respect for fundamental rights within the member states themselves. Yet citizens of states where the rights are respected could hardly accept laws made by Union institutions containing representatives from states where they are not. The prospect that several new democracies will soon join the Union spurred governments to guard against this possibility. So the treaty affirmed that the Union is 'founded on the principles of liberty, democracy, respect for human rights and fundamental freedoms, and the rule of law, principles which are common to the member states'; and it went on to provide that, in the event of a 'serious and persistent breach' of these principles, a member state could be deprived of some of its rights under the treaty, including voting rights.

In response to concerns that the Union needs to do more to attract the support of its citizens, a Charter of Fundamental Rights was also drafted, in parallel with the IGC 2000, by a Convention of MEPs, members of the states' parliaments, and government representatives. A major issue is whether people claiming infringement of these rights should have recourse to the courts, but the European Council at Nice, while 'welcoming' the Charter, did not include it in the Treaty.

Apart from the question of rights, the system for governing the Union, with its complex mix of intergovernmental and federal elements, makes decision-making difficult and a satisfactory relationship between the institutions and the citizens hard to achieve. Yet unless the citizens develop sufficient support for the Union alongside that for their own states, the states' electorates could become a centrifugal force leading to disintegration. The future enlargement to over twenty, probably eventually over thirty, states will intensify the difficulties. While reforms agreed by the IGC 2000 should be of help, severe doubts remain as to whether the institutions will be effective and democratic enough for the enlarged Union to be successful and to attract the citizens' support, unless there is further reform.

Chapter 4
Single market, single currency

While peace among the member states remained at the heart of the Community's purpose, from the second half of the 1950s a large common market became the focus for its action. The strength of the US economy was a striking example of the success of such a market; the Germans and the Dutch wanted liberal trade; and the French accepted the common market in industrial goods provided it was accompanied by the agricultural common market that would favour their own exports.

The idea of a large common market had a dynamic that endured through the subsequent decades, because it reflected the growing reality of economic interdependence. As technologies developed, and with them economies of scale, more and more firms of all sizes needed access to a large, secure market; and for the health of the economy and the benefit of the consumers, the market had to be big enough to provide scope for competition, even among the largest firms. So as the European economies developed, the EEC's original project, centred on abolition of tariffs in a customs union, was succeeded in the 1980s by the single market programme, then in the 1990s by the single currency.

There were both economic and political motives for each of the three projects: the benefits of economic rationality; and the consolidation of the Community system as a framework for peaceful relations among the member states. Economics and politics were also both involved in the substance and outcomes of the projects, because the integration of modern economies requires a framework of law, and hence common political and judicial institutions. Nor would success in either the economic or the political field alone have been enough to sustain the Community. There had to be success in both, which the customs union and the single market both achieved. It was also a combination of economic and political motives that secured the launch of the single currency, though not yet the participation of all member states.

The single market

Tariffs and import quotas were, in the 1950s, still the principal barriers to trade. The international process of reducing them began under American leadership in the Gatt (General Agreement on Tariffs and Trade). But the member states of the Community wanted to do more. The result was the EEC's customs union, abolishing tariff and quota barriers to their mutual trade, and creating a common external tariff.

Customs union, competition policy

Tariffs and quotas on trade between the member states were removed by stages between 1958 and 1968. Industry responded positively and trade across the frontiers grew rapidly, more than doubling during the decade.

While tariffs and quotas were the main distortions impeding trade, they were not the only ones. The Community was also given powers to forbid restrictive practices and abuse of dominant positions in the private sector. The treaty gave the task to the Commission, without intervention by member state governments; and in 1989 the Commission was also given the power to control mergers and acquisitions big enough to pose a threat to competition in the Community. Armed with these powers, the Commission has done much to discourage anti-competitive behaviour. Thus in 1992 the Commission fined Volkswagen ecu 102 million,* later reduced to €90 million on appeal to the Court of First Instance, for requiring its dealers in Italy to refuse to sell cars to foreign buyers – who came mostly from Germany and Austria where the cars were priced much higher. Because of the volume of work, the Commission has recently sought to return some of these responsibilities to the member states' competition authorities. But there has been pressure from business interests to prevent this, because they find it convenient to have the Commission as a 'one-stop shop'.

Unfair competition can also take the form of subsidies given by a member state government to a firm or sector (in the EU jargon 'state aids'), enabling it to undercut efficient competitors and undermine their viability. The Commission has been given the power to forbid such subsidies. But it has been harder to control governments than firms. The Commission has been able to enforce some difficult decisions on reluctant governments; but especially in the 1970s, after it had been weakened by de Gaulle and with the economies hard hit by recession, it could do little to stem the rising tide of subsidies.

Along with the subsidies, non-tariff barriers proliferated in those years, becoming the main obstacle to trade between member states. One reason was technological progress, generating complex regulations differing from one state to another. More important was pressure for protection from those who were suffering from the prevailing 'stagflation'. The European economy was indeed in bad shape, vividly evoked by the term eurosclerosis. A way out was sought; and the Commission, together with leading business interests, persuaded governments that a programme to complete the Community's internal market was required.

* The ecu (European Currency Unit) was a forerunner of the euro, on which the value of the euro was based. € is the symbol for the euro.

State aids to manufacturing in selected EU states, 1986 and 1996
(percentage of GDP)

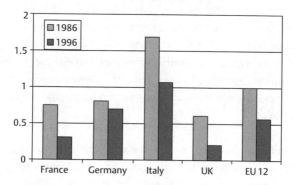

Note: In 1996, the figure for the EU15 was 0.54%

Programme to complete the single market by 1992

With the success of the internal tariff disarmament in the 1960s in mind, some business leaders and members of the Commission's staff worked on the idea of a programme to remove the non-tariff barriers. When Delors became the Commission's President in 1985, he fastened onto this idea as the only major initiative that would be supported by the governments of all the member states: the majority because of its economic merits and the political aim of 'relaunching the Community' after two rather stagnant decades; Mrs Thatcher because of economic liberalization alone. But she did the Community the service of nominating the highly capable Lord Cockfield, who had been trade minister in her Cabinet, as a Commissioner to work with Delors on the project.

Delors and Cockfield put the project to the European Council in June 1985. Whereas the programme for eliminating tariffs in the 1960s could be specified in the treaty in the form of percentage reductions, the removal of non-tariff barriers required a vast programme of Community legislation. Frontier formalities and discrimination resulting from standards and regulations, from public purchasing, and from anomalies in indirect taxation all had to be tackled. The Commission published a White Paper specifying that some 300 measures would have to be enacted and proposing a timetable for completing the programme within eight years. This was approved by the European Council and incorporated in the Single European Act, making completion of the programme by the end of 1992 a treaty obligation.

The removal of non-tariff barriers was already implicit in the Rome Treaty, which prohibited 'all measures having equivalent effect' to import quotas. But because the practice of voting by unanimity had impeded the legislative process, the Single Act provided for qualified majority voting on most of the measures needed to complete the programme. The Commission also reduced the legislative burden by building on the principle of mutual recognition that the Court had established by its judgment in the Cassis de Dijon case, and by delegating decisions on much of the detail to existing standards institutes. Nevertheless, the single market remained a huge enterprise, surely one of the greatest programmes of legislation liberalizing trade in the history of the world.

It was an outstanding success. The latter half of the 1980s was a period of economic regeneration in the Community. While one cannot be sure how much of that was due to the single market programme, economic research has given it at least some of the credit. The programme certainly contributed to the recovery by generating positive views of business prospects as well as stimulating trade, together with structural reform exemplified by a spate of cross-border mergers. The industrially less-developed states, Greece, Portugal, Spain, and at that time Ireland, fearing they would be damaged by stronger competitors, had secured a doubling of the structural funds to help them adjust; and they too,

Non-tariff barriers

When the Community was founded, the main barriers to trade were tariffs and quotas, and the Rome Treaty provided for their abolition in trade between member states. The Treaty also banned 'measures having equivalent effect', i.e. other barriers, generally known as non-tariff barriers (NTBs), which might not be expressly designed to limit trade but would actually have that effect. These include divergent standards or regulations on goods and services in the different states; frontier controls on goods and people; some discriminatory indirect taxes; and national preference by public purchasing authorities and state enterprises. The Treaty also provided for control of government subsidies to firms or individual sectors, to prevent unfair competition with more efficient enterprises in other member states.

As technologies developed and the economies became more complex, NTBs proliferated; and in the recessions of the 1970s governments resorted to them and to subsidies as protective devices. This led to the project to complete the single market through a vast programme of legislation to tackle NTBs. The bulk of the programme was completed as planned by the end of 1992, though barriers in some sectors have not yet been eliminated.

assisted by this and by the expanding Community economy, benefited from the programme.

Politically, the single market has enjoyed a remarkable degree of approval across the spectrum from federalists to eurosceptics. It has been a classic example of a purpose that is, as the treaty's article on subsidiarity puts it, 'by reason of scale . . . better achieved by the

Community'. The legislative framework has guaranteed producers a very large market and given the consumer a reasonable assurance of competitive behaviour among them. The Commission, Council, and Parliament were strengthened by their successful output, comprising a large part of the vast 'acquis', as the jargon puts it, of Community legislation; and the role of the Court was accordingly enhanced.

The programme has been largely completed but significant gaps remain. Most member states have been slow in removing discrimination from their public purchasing. Some discriminatory regulations still, in 2000, remained in a few important sectors of the economy, including air transport, electric power, telecommunications, and financial services. But while France remained reluctant to accept a date for completing the single market in air transport and electric power, the European Council agreed in March 2000 that telecommunications would be completely liberalized by the end of 2001 and financial services by 2005. There had, however, already been substantial liberalization of the latter in the course of the 1992 programme, including a key element in the approach to the single currency: the free movement of capital.

The single currency

A monetary union requires that money in all its forms can move freely across the frontiers between member states and that changes of exchange rates between them are abolished. The single market programme went far to fulfil the first requirement and the Exchange Rate Mechanism prepared the ground for the second.

The ERM and monetary stability

The Exchange Rate Mechanism (ERM) was established in 1979, after the abortive attempt to move to monetary union in the 1970s. It required the central banks to intervene in the currency markets to keep fluctuations of their mutual exchange rates within narrow bands; and by the end of the 1980s it had, with the German Bundesbank as anchor, achieved a strong record of monetary stability. Here again, Britain stood aside at the start, only to join in 1990, at too high a rate and without the experience of the preceding decade of co-operation. In September 1992 currency turmoil forced the pound out of the ERM on what became known as Black Wednesday, making monetary integration a traumatic subject for many British politicians.

The ERM had the opposite effect in other member states. Most politicians as well as business organizations, having experienced the benefits of stable exchange rates, favoured the single currency. So did most trade unions. The costs of exchange-rate transactions, estimated at ecu 13–19 billion a year, which bear particularly hard on individuals and smaller firms, would be eliminated. But removal of the longer term risks of exchange-rate instability would be the main economic benefit, definitively eliminating the exchange-rate risk, not just from trade but also, most significantly, from cross-border investments and from those that depend on reliable access to the Union-wide market: both of growing importance for a dynamic European economy.

Almost all the governments supported the single currency project, on grounds that reflected long-standing attitudes towards the Community. The most powerful commitment was in France, where a tradition of support for exchange-rate stability was bolstered by the desire to share in the control of a European central bank and thus recover some of the monetary autonomy that had in practice been lost to the Bundesbank. The French had also long wanted to equip Europe to challenge the global hegemony of the dollar; and in 1990 the single currency, already a keystone of the French political project for anchoring Germany in a united Europe, became for France an urgent necessity to respond to German unification. Other member states, apart from Denmark and the UK, accepted both political and economic arguments. For Germany, however, while the political motive for accepting the single currency as a French condition of unification was decisive, there were still reservations about replacing the deutschmark, with its well-earned strength and stability, by an unproven currency.

The success of the Bundesbank in securing monetary stability had demonstrated the merits of Germany's monetary arrangements. So other governments were ready to accept the German model for monetary union. For Germans, with their doubts about giving up the deutschmark, this was a *sine qua non*. They also continued to insist that monetary union alone was not enough, but that 'economic union' was required as well, with macroeconomic policies conducive to monetary stability.

The aim of economic and monetary union

The Maastricht Treaty, in providing for economic and monetary union (Emu), established the European Central Bank (ECB) to be, like the Bundesbank, completely independent. The ECB and the central banks of the member states are together called the European System of Central Banks (ESCB). The six members of the ECB's Executive Board, together with the governors of the other central banks, comprise the Governing Council of the ECB; and none of these banks, nor any member of their decision-making organs, is to take instructions from any other body. The 'primary objective' of the ESCB is 'to maintain price stability' though, subject to that overriding requirement, it is also to support the Community's 'general economic policies'. The ECB is to have the sole right to authorize the issue of notes, and to approve the quantity of coins issued by the states' mints. In response to German preference, the single currency was named the euro, rather than the French-sounding ecu.

In order to ensure that only states which had achieved monetary stability should participate in the euro, five 'convergence criteria' were established regarding rates of inflation and of interest, ceilings for budget deficits and for total public debt, and stability of exchange rates.

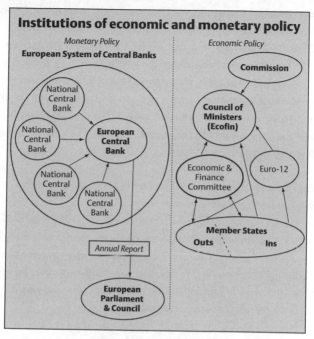

Institutions of economic and monetary policy

Monetary Policy

European System of Central Banks

- National Central Bank
- National Central Bank
- National Central Bank
- National Central Bank
- **European Central Bank**

Annual Report

European Parliament & Council

Economic Policy

Commission

Council of Ministers (Ecofin)

Economic & Finance Committee

Euro-12

Member States

Outs   Ins

14. The euro: notes and coins.

Budget deficits, for example, were not to exceed 3 per cent of GDP and public debt was to be limited to 60 per cent of GDP, unless it was 'sufficiently diminishing' and approaching the limit 'at a satisfactory pace'. Only states that had satisfied the criteria were to be allowed to participate; and once again, stages and a timetable were fixed, in order to give at least a minimum number of states the time to do so. Others were to have 'derogations' until they satisfied the criteria, while the British and Danes negotiated opt-outs allowing them to remain outside unless they should choose to join.

In the first stage all states were to accept the ERM, which Britain briefly did before being ejected by market forces. In the second stage they were to make enough progress to satisfy the convergence criteria. The third stage was to begin by January 1999 with the 'irrevocable fixing of exchange rates' among the participating states, leading by 2002 to the introduction of the single currency. The euro could meanwhile be used for transactions not requiring the use of notes or coins, and would replace the participants' currencies entirely in 2002.

Ins and outs

When the convergence criteria were set, it was thought that six or seven of the thirteen states without opt-outs would satisfy them by 1999. In the event the will to participate was so strong that there were eleven: Austria, Belgium, Finland, France, Germany, Ireland, Luxembourg, Netherlands, Portugal, and Spain, together with Italy which, against all expectations, managed under Prime Minister Prodi to do so. Fear that the most federalist of all the member states could be excluded from such a crucial development moved Italian politicians to adapt their behaviour accordingly. Greece, the only state that had to accept a derogation, was likewise determined to satisfy the criteria and had joined on 1 January 2001. The British and Swedish governments were still intending to hold referenda on the question of participation, but in September 2000 the Danish voters rejected it by 53 per cent to 47 per cent.

In Britain, the question of participation evoked intense political conflict. Mrs Thatcher gave vent to her feelings by crying 'no . . . no . . . no!' to the House of Commons. Her successor John Major negotiated the opt-out at Maastricht; and all three major parties promised they would not apply to join the euro without a referendum. Though some of the most senior Conservatives were committed to entry 'when the economic conditions were right', the Conservative Party turned increasingly hostile and William Hague, as Leader of the Opposition from 1997, introduced the policy that a Conservative government would not seek to join the euro during the course of the next parliament, following elections due at the latest by May 2002 but likely to be held in 2001.

Opinion polls showed that the public too was sceptical about the euro. The new Labour government favoured joining in principle but subject to its own five conditions. Three of these were the expected effects on British investment; on financial services and the City of London; and on growth, stability, and jobs. A fourth was sufficient flexibility in member states' economies to make necessary adjustment possible without adjusting exchange rates, thus enabling Emu to be a success. The fifth was convergence of Britain's economic cycle with that of the euro-zone. The *Financial Times* has called the first four 'essay questions', which the government can if it wishes answer positively. But 'cyclical convergence' has more substance: Britain's interest rates will have to be close enough to those of the euro-zone in order to avoid a shock to the British economy; and the pound will have to be exchanged for the euro at an acceptable rate.

The Confederation of British Industry and most of the larger firms supported the government's policy; the Trades Union Congress, worried about the effect of exclusion on jobs, wanted entry as soon as possible. Most of the press was against. Campaigns were mounted on both sides of the argument. Studies showed that, with nearly 60 per cent of British exports of goods going to other member states, over three million jobs depended on that trade. So the pro-euro

Brown's five points

British government statement on the euro after its launch in January 1999:

'The Maastricht Treaty allows the UK to choose if and when it wants to join the single currency. The Government has decided that the UK economy is not ready for us to join on 1 January 1999. However, the Government supports the principle of joining the single currency, if that is in the national economic interest. It does not expect that to be the case during this Parliament. Instead, the Government is making the necessary preparations so that we have the option of joining the single currency early in the next Parliament (which will start no later than Spring 2002). If the Government decided that the UK should join, the British people would have the final say in a referendum.'

How will the Government decide?

The UK did not join EMU on 1 January 1999. Any Government decision to join the single currency at a future date will be based on the national economic interest. The Government will examine the following questions:

- would joining EMU create better conditions for firms making long-term decisions to invest in the United Kingdom?
- how would adopting the single currency affect our financial services?
- are business cycles and economic structures compatible so that we and others in Europe could live comfortably with euro interest rates on a permanent basis?
- if problems do emerge, is there sufficient flexibility to deal with them?
- will joining EMU help to promote higher growth, stability and a lasting increase in jobs?'

organization, Britain in Europe, could argue that prospects for those jobs would be less good and some would be at risk without British adoption of the euro. Investment in the UK, particularly the 'inward investment' by foreign firms, would be discouraged. British influence in the EU would decline; and the arguments against the euro could launch Britain on a slippery slope towards exit from the Union itself, with disastrous consequences for jobs and the economy. Business for Sterling, campaigning against participation, declared its support for the single market but not the single currency. It argued that the euro-zone's 'one size fits all' monetary policy would not fit Britain and would thus cause inflationary or deflationary pressures, on the grounds that Britain's economic structures differed too much from those of the Continent. Many opponents of the euro took its fall against the dollar in 1999 as evidence of a fundamental weakness; they have criticized the independence of the ECB as a lack of accountability; and they regard Emu as a step towards a 'centralized superstate'. Most of these arguments concern particular aspects of general questions posed by Emu for all the member states.

Questions raised by Emu

Following the introduction of the euro, four major questions need to be addressed: the macroeconomic effect on the Union and the several states; external monetary relations; accountability; and the political consequences.

The argument about Emu's macroeconomic effects on the euro-zone has followed the classic dichotomy between the prevention of inflation and of deflation. As in fixing the convergence criteria, the strength and reputation of the deutschmark ensured that prevention of inflation was built into the system. In addition to the independence of all the member states' central banks, the Maastricht Treaty required that the limits of 3 per cent of GDP for budget deficits and 60 per cent of GDP for public debts continue to apply. The merit of these rules was widely accepted; and Britain and Denmark, despite their opt-outs from the euro, agreed that they should apply in all the member states. In the language of subsidiarity, this was justified because inflationary behaviour by one state would have an 'external effect' on others by spilling over into their economies; and excessive borrowing to finance deficits would push up interest rates throughout the Union.

Unemployment had persisted for some years at rates around 10 per cent in member states except Britain, the Netherlands, and Austria; and rates of growth had been slow. Pressure grew to counterbalance the anti-inflationary policies with action favouring employment and growth. This was supported by the left-of-centre governments that had been elected in Britain and France just before the final negotiation on the Amsterdam Treaty, which contained a new section on employment; and a Stability and Growth Pact was agreed at the same time. Germany's right-of-centre government was still in place and insisted that the pact firm up the anti-inflationary provisions, stipulating that budget deficits should be reduced to zero during periods of economic upswing and that governments failing to meet the deficit or debt criterion could be fined. But there was also provision for action favouring employment, largely through 'bench-marking' progress on measures taken by member states rather than through legislation by the Community itself.

Gerhard Schröder was soon to replace Helmut Kohl as Chancellor and the new German government began to favour more expansionary policies, though without, after Oskar Lafontaine's short spell as Finance Minister, abandoning the traditional German attachment to stability. There were calls for the ECB, whose President Wim Duisenberg is a tough disinflationist, to cut interest rates more than it thought prudent; and he in turn, together with the Commission, called on the governments to achieve that result by reducing their deficits and hence their demand for money from the capital markets. But while there was argument about macroeconomic policy, there was, after Lafontaine's departure, no deep divergence.

Stability and Growth Pact

The European Council at Amsterdam in 1997 agreed not only on the new treaty but also on the Stability and Growth Pact, for stronger coordination of member states' policies on public-sector deficits. The medium-term objective is budgets 'close to balance or in surplus'. There can be penalties for a state that does not rectify a deficit which has risen above the 3 per cent ceiling, unless the cause is a natural disaster or a recession causing a fall in real GDP of at least 0.75 per cent. The aim is to prevent one or more member states from exporting inflation and monetary instability to the Union as a whole by lax financial management.

Were the Council to decide that a member state's deficit had risen above the 3 per cent ceiling and should not be exempted on those grounds, they would recommend how best it should tackle the deficit. Should it fail to do so within a year, the Pact 'urges' the Council to require the state to hand over a non-interest bearing deposit, and to convert the deposit into a fine if after two years the excessive deficit has not been corrected.

At the same time the Amsterdam Treaty sought to meet concerns about unemployment through its new chapter on employment (see box below on p. 98).

Much discussion among economists about problems that may arise has concerned the possibility of 'asymmetric shocks', having a differential impact on the several member states. The preferred response is the provision of loans to give such states time to adjust; and a special fund for the purpose has been suggested. Responding, as in the case of the single market, to the longer term asymmetry between stronger and weaker economies, the Community again increased the budget for the structural funds and established a Cohesion Fund for trans-European transport infrastructure and environmental projects.

Debate in Britain has focused, rather, on asymmetry between member states in the degree of flexibility of their labour and product markets, seen as a necessary means of adjustment when the exchange rate can no longer be used: hence the inclusion of sufficient flexibility in member states as one of the government's five conditions for participation, on the grounds that the euro will not otherwise be successful. Mrs Thatcher's government swept away many rigidities in the 1980s. But the French growth rate and Germany's export performance remain impressive and they, like other member states, have embarked on a process of structural reform. It seems unlikely that their performance will be poor enough to render them unable to cope with problems of adjustment.

There is also concern about differing economic cycles within the euro-zone. Interest rates at levels that suit the average will not be optimal for states with inflationary pressures above or below the average; and this is a downside to set against the general benefits of Emu. But the suggestion that the British cycle has to follow that of the United States, and so differs structurally from the average in the euro-zone, does not fit well with the facts that nearly 60 per cent of British exports of goods go to the EU, compared with 13 per cent to the USA, and that cross-Channel investment has been growing fast. Nor is the economic cycle a force of nature that cannot be influenced by government policy aiming at adequate convergence.

It has been suggested that the euro's fall against the dollar in 1999–2000 reflects a basic structural weakness in the European economy. But such fluctuations in exchange rates between the dollar and European currencies have been commonplace in previous years. The tide in the markets will turn, central banks will decide to increase their holdings of the euro as a reserve currency, and the euro will move in the opposite direction. The fundamental question is how to devise an international mechanism that can reduce such fluctuations, as the ERM did in Europe. The existence of the euro gives the EU the opportunity to negotiate such a system on level terms with the USA, as the common external tariff enabled the Community to negotiate trade liberalization. But whereas there are strong institutions for internal management of the euro, the arrangements for conducting external monetary policy are weak. The euro makes it possible to create a more balanced international financial system; and the Europeans need to get their act together if they are to do so.

The independence of a central bank being a new experience for all except the Germans, the question of the ECB's accountability has also been raised. The treaty requires it to address an annual report to the Community institutions; its President has to present the report in person to the Council and the Parliament; and the President and other members of the ECB's Board attend meetings of the Parliament's relevant committees. The system is similar to that of the United States, save that the Joint Economic Policy Committee of the Congress has over the years become a powerful body disposing of a big budget to provide it with the necessary economic analysis and advice. The European Parliament's Finance Committee should surely move in that direction.

This leads to the question of the implications of Emu for the EU's powers and institutions. It is often suggested that far-reaching tax harmonization will have to follow. But the principle of subsidiarity requires that member states choose the pattern of their own taxes unless this has an 'external effect' on other member states. Thus minimum rates of added-value tax and excise taxes were fixed, with the agreement of Britain's then Conservative government, as part of the single market programme, in order to prevent unfair competition should a state adopt unduly low rates. Emu strengthens the case for similar treatment of taxes that affect competition in the capital markets. But beyond that there is no need to harmonize tax rates. There is a case for a fund for use on the infrequent occasions when there are serious asymmetric shocks; and there is a strong case for reforming the institutions so as to enable the Union to conduct an effective external monetary policy. But in general the EU has, with the single market, the single currency, and its budget, the main instruments of economic policy to be found in federal systems. It does not need much more.

Another suggestion is that Emu will lead inevitably to a federal state. But a federal state has to have power over armed forces; and this does not follow from the adoption of the euro. The argument about defence integration, which is addressed later, is a different one. As regards strengthening the institutions and making them more democratic, that is already desirable, with or without the single currency; and it will, with the prospect of enlargement ahead, become essential if the Union is to be capable of satisfying its citizens' needs and avoid the risk of disintegration. The euro adds to the case for institutional reform. But it is far from providing the principal motive. The forthcoming enlargement is a great deal more critical.

Chapter 5
Agriculture, regions, budget: conflicts over who gets what

The single market is a positive-sum game. Because it enhances productivity in the economy, there is benefit for most people, whether they take it in the form of consuming more or working less. But alongside the majority who gain, there will be some who lose, or at least fear they will lose, from the opening of markets to new competition; and these may demand compensation for agreeing to participate in the new arrangements. Such compensation usually has implications for the Community budget and looks like a zero-sum game, which can lead to conflict between those who pay and those who receive, even if the package of compensation and competition, taken together, benefits both parties. The first major example was the inclusion of agriculture in the EEC's common market.

Agriculture

The opening of the Community's market to trade in manufactures was, when the EEC was founded, a relatively simple matter of eliminating tariffs and quotas by stages. But tariff and quota disarmament was only a small part of the problem of creating an agricultural common market. All European countries managed their agricultural markets with complex devices such as subsidies and price supports to ensure adequate incomes for farmers and security of food supplies. So a common market for agriculture would have to be a complicated managed market for the Community, to replace those of the member states. It would have been simpler to confine the common market to industry. But the French feared the prospect of German industrial competition and, having a competitive agricultural sector, insisted that the Community market be opened to agriculture too.

High prices and Thatcher's 'money back'

The result was the common agricultural policy, with prices of the main products supported at levels decided by the Council of agriculture ministers, through variable levies on imports from outside the Community and purchase of surplus production into storage at the support level. Farmers' incomes were bolstered by high prices paid by the consumer, together with subsidies from the Community's taxpayers to finance the surpluses that the high prices evoked.

Consumers in the Community's six founding states had experienced similar systems and were used to high prices. The British, having espoused free trade in the nineteenth century, were accustomed to cheap food, with large imports from the USA and the Commonwealth and with subsidies paid to British farmers to keep their prices down to world levels. So adoption of the common agricultural policy (CAP) when Britain joined the Community increased the price of food; and as well as being unpleasant for consumers, the high food prices were the main cause of Britain's problem with the Community budget. For the difference between the Community prices and the world prices of Britain's large imports of foodstuffs from overseas was paid as import levies into the Community budget; and the bulk of expenditure from the budget consisted of subsidies to continental farmers, with relatively little going to the small British farm sector. Britain's net contribution to the budget was expected to rise after a transitional period to some 0.75 per cent of British national income. So it was agreed during the entry negotiations that, should 'unacceptable situations' arise, 'equitable solutions' would be found to deal with them.

But when Mrs Thatcher became Prime Minister in 1979, there had been no such solution. For nearly five years she fought a bitter battle, blocking much other Community business, as her method of what she called 'getting our money back'. Matters came to a head in 1984, when the accumulation of stocks such as 'butter mountains' and 'wine lakes' had cost so much that the Community needed to raise the ceiling for its revenue from taxation; and this required unanimous agreement by the member states. So a deal was done, with agreement on a higher ceiling for tax resources allocated to the Community and an annual rebate for Britain at around two-thirds of its net contribution. At the same time a step was taken to reform the CAP, but only a modest step, because attention had been focused on the questions of the rebate and the tax resources.

Stages of reform

The CAP lumbered on, accumulating further costly surpluses, until 1988 when the money ran out again. This time the financial interests of member states prevailed. With the division of the Council into functional formations, the decisions of the Council of agriculture ministers on prices of farm products had determined the level of the bulk of Community expenditure, over which the Council of finance ministers had little say. Since the resulting bill had to be paid out of the Community's tax resources, the agriculture ministers were in effect deciding on the rate of tax paid by the citizens to the Community. Financial control had to be established and the European Council agreed in 1988 on a package of measures, proposed by Delors, which introduced a 'financial perspective' setting limits for the main headings of the Community's expenditure during the five years 1988–92. The growth of spending on agriculture was restricted to less than three-quarters of the rate of growth of the total.

While this took some of the heat out of the conflict over money, a serious reform of the CAP was still required. By 1992 the Commissioner responsible for agriculture was Ray MacSharry, a former Irish minister.

Share of budget spent on CAP, 1970–2000

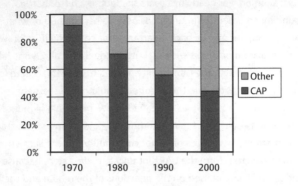

He grasped the nettle and, outmanœuvring the opposing interests, secured a cut of 15 per cent in the support price for beef and nearly one-third for cereals. The current levels of expenditure were not reduced, because farmers were compensated with income supports, including 'set-aside' payments for leaving cultivated land to lie fallow. But the measures removed the expansionary dynamic from the CAP and prepared the ground for further reform.

The cost of the CAP remained a heavy burden for the Community, with half the budget going to support a sector that employs less than 5 per cent of the working population, much of it for a small minority of the bigger and richer farmers. By the end of the 1990s, moreover, enlargement to the East was approaching, with the prospect of a large farm population likely to produce big surpluses if paid present EU prices. It had also been agreed that the first round of negotiations in the newly established World Trade Organization (WTO) would limit subsidies for agricultural exports; and the EU has to deliver its side of the bargain if it is to promote its interest in a liberal world trading system. So the Commission's White Paper, *Agenda 2000*, contained proposals for CAP reform, among other measures to prepare the Union for enlargement. At the European Council in Berlin in March 1999, however, which took the decisions on *Agenda 2000*, President Chirac threw his weight against some of the price cuts proposed for agricultural products, and Chancellor Schröder, in order to avoid the risk of impairing the Franco-German relationship, secured agreement to settle for less. Though the cuts of 15 per cent for cereals and 20 per cent over a three-year period for beef were substantial, the costly regime for milk products was not seriously tackled. A further round of cuts will be required.

So the long story of inadequate CAP reform, which has led to such bitter quarrels about the distribution of costs and benefits among the member states, will have to last a few more years. The original British concerns, reflecting the interests of consumers, of taxpayers, and of international trade partners that provide essential export markets, have turned out to be the interests of the majority of EU citizens too. But the British, and Mrs Thatcher in particular, generally presented their case in terms of national interest. The story might have been less painfully long had they tried harder to persuade their partners that this British interest was also the interest of the large majority of Europeans.

Cohesion and structural funds

The 'cohesion policy', the other big item of expenditure in the Community's budget, has been a happier experience than the CAP. It stems from fears in member states with weaker economies that they would lose in free competition within the Community. When the customs union, the single market, and the single currency were established, funds were provided to assist their economic development so that they would co-operate in these new ventures and become prosperous partners: hence the word 'cohesion'.

Italy and Britain: Social Fund and Regional Development Fund

The first such provision was for the Social Fund, included at Italy's request in the Treaty of Rome. Italy's economy was the weakest among the six founding states and Italians feared they would suffer from the liberalization of trade. They wanted a fund to help their workforce to adapt; and their demand was met, though on quite a small scale.

The motive for establishing the European Regional Development Fund (ERDF) was somewhat different. By the time of British accession in 1973, Britain's economic performance had fallen behind those of the six founder states; and there was the prospect of the big net contribution for the CAP. Britain had its share and more of regions with economic difficulties, but other member states had theirs too. Edward Heath's government, which had negotiated British accession, had the sound idea that a fund for regional assistance would both respond to a general interest and be of particular value to Britain, not only assisting its regional development but also reducing its net contribution to the Community budget. But though the fund was established soon after British entry, it was then too small to have much impact, partly because agreement to spend money was harder to reach in the hard times of the 1970s, partly because Germany was becoming resistant to further expansion of its role as the principal contributor to the Community's budget, and partly because elections had brought in a Labour government that lacked commitment to the idea.

The third of what became known as the 'structural funds', in order to underline that their aim was not just to redistribute money but rather to improve economic performance in the weaker parts of the Community's economy, was the 'Guidance Section' of the European Agricultural Guarantee and Guidance Fund (EAGGF). The Guarantee Section, which finances the subsidies for price support, far outweighs the Guidance Section whose purpose is to help farmers carry out structural change. But the three structural funds, though at first small, grew steadily and were available to respond to the demand for a major expansion in the 1980s when the Community was enlarged to the south.

Southern enlargement and structural funds

When Spain, Portugal, and Greece joined the Community, their average incomes were far below those of the other member states save Ireland, which before its phenomenal growth in the 1990s was at a similar level. These four countries, led by Spain, demanded a major increase in the structural funds. They evoked a ready response from Delors, who in the run-up to Spanish and Portuguese entry was steering the single market project through the Intergovernmental Conference that produced the Single European Act. He was strongly motivated by the idea of social justice; and, though the governments had various views on that subject, it was evident that four discontented states could cause difficulties for the passage of the single market legislation. So the Single Act contained an article on 'economic and social cohesion'; Delors proposed that the budget for the structural funds be doubled in the financial perspective for 1988–92; and this was accepted by the European Council.

A similar problem emerged when it was decided to embark on Emu, with the same four states seeking a similar expansion of the structural funds. This time Delors secured an increase of two-fifths in the allocation for the period 1993–9; and the Maastricht Treaty provided for the establishment of the Cohesion Fund, to support projects in the fields of the environment and transport infrastructure. By 2000 the budget for the funds was €32 billion.

The four states for which the expansion of the structural funds was designed have performed for the most part well, with the Portuguese and particularly the Irish economy growing faster than the Union's average, Spain also successful, and Greece, after faltering for a number of years, meeting the Maastricht convergence criteria in 2000. While it is not possible to say how much of this can be attributed to the structural funds, their contributions can hardly have been negligible, given that Ireland received in the mid-1990s the equivalent of some

Structural funds and objectives

Since the early 1970s, the Community has developed its regional policies around a set of funds and objectives. These were reformed in 1999.

The Structural Funds now comprise:

- the European Regional Development Fund (ERDF) – the main fund, with annual budget recently around €13 billion;
- the European Social Fund (ESF) – concerned with re-training workers, €7.5 billion a year;
- the Guidance section of the European Agricultural Guarantee and Guidance Fund (EAGGF) – used for structural reforms in rural areas, €4 billion a year;
- Financial Instrument for Fisheries Guidance (FIFG);
- Cohesion Fund – aimed at poorer member states, this fund was created at Maastricht to develop projects in the environment and infrastructure: about €3 billion a year.

Spending is focused on three key objectives:

- areas with GDP per head less than 75% of the EU average – two-thirds of funding goes on this, covering about 20% of the population;
- areas undergoing economic and social conversion or facing structural problems (like coal-mining or ship-building areas) – some 18% of the population will benefit from this;
- not related to specific areas, supports adaptation and modernization of education, training, and employment policies.

3 per cent of its GDP from them, Greece and Portugal 4 per cent each, and Spain 2 per cent.

Although the objectives of the structural funds had been focused on help for regions where development was 'lagging behind', responding largely to the needs of these four states, 'declining industrial areas' had been added, thus pleasing Northern states which have been the main contributors to the budget. 'Rural areas' were also added as diversification of employment opportunities in the countryside became an element of CAP reform; and 'employment and industrial change' was included in response to worries about Europe's competitive position in an era of global technological advance. The result has been that the structural funds have targeted areas including over half the EU's population, rather than concentrating on the minority of hardest cases. One aim of the Commission's *Agenda 2000* proposals was to reduce the degree of dispersal in order to free resources to deal with higher priorities.

Preparing for Eastern enlargement

A major priority was to help prepare the Central and East European countries for accession. With a majority of member states now significant net contributors to the budget and public finances under pressure with the introduction of the euro, the Commission was constrained to stay below the ceiling of 1.27 per cent of Union GDP for its total tax revenue; and the main existing recipients from the structural funds, led again by Spain, resisted any reduction in their own receipts. Given those limits, the financial perspective agreed by the Berlin European Council in 1999 allocated a sum rising to €12 billion by 2006 for new member states, or just over a third of the total for structural funds in that year. It is doubtful whether this will be enough. Average incomes in the first wave of five Central and East European states negotiating accession are less than half the EU average, whereas the proportion in all member states that joined in the past was over half. For all the second wave except Slovakia it is still below one-third. The Union will suffer if there is too much disparity among the states; and the structural funds may have to take at least part of the strain.

So far, however, the cohesion policy has, unlike the CAP, been relatively harmonious. This doubtless reflects partly the principle of social justice that permeates the polities of the member states, partly the fact that there have been benefits for a lot of people in all of them. But harmony has not been a notable characteristic of the history of the budget as a whole.

The budget

With agriculture now accounting for under half of EU expenditure and cohesion somewhat over one-third, the two together, with their powerfully redistributive effects, account for four-fifths. The cost of administration in the Union's institutions comes to less than 5 per cent of the total and the remainder goes to finance a range of internal and external policies. A major item of redistribution outside the budget is the rebate to reduce the British net contribution, which amounted in 1999 to £3.1 billion and is paid direct to Britain by the other member states.

The total expenditure in the budget for 2000 was €89.6 billion, or 1.13 per cent of Union GDP. This has to remain below 1.27 per cent of GNP unless that ceiling is increased by a decision ratified by all the member states; and the financial perspective for the years 2000–6 keeps spending below 1.20 per cent of GNP in each year.

'Own resources'

Unlike international organizations that depend on contributions from their member states, the EU's revenue from taxes is a legal requirement under the treaty, subject, like other treaty obligations, to the authority of the Court of Justice. This is to prevent member states from holding

Breakdown of budget expenditure, 2000

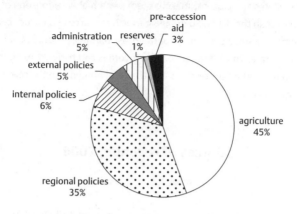

the Union to ransom by withholding contributions. The consequences of such behaviour are demonstrated by the financial state of the United Nations, weakened for many years by the refusal of Congress to sanction payment of the due US contribution – ironically enough, since the failure of American states to pay their due contributions in the 1780s under the Articles of Confederation was a powerful argument in favour of the US federal constitution. The same argument influenced the EC's founding fathers to make the payment of tax revenue to the Community a legal obligation. The EU has no physical means of enforcement should a member state not hand over the money. But the rule of law has been of sufficient value to the member states to be respected by them.

Initially the EEC's tax revenue, called in the treaty 'own resources' to underline the point that they belong to the Community not the states, comprised the takings from customs duties and agricultural import levies. But these were not enough to pay for the CAP and the Community was allocated a share of value-added tax at a rate of 1 per cent of the value of the goods and services on which VAT is levied.

A major objection to these indirect taxes was that they bear hard on the poorer states and citizens, making them pay a higher proportion of incomes than the richer. So in 1988 a fourth resource was introduced, in the form of a small percentage of the gross national product of each member state. This is proportional to incomes and by 1999 accounted for about half the EU's revenue. But the total outcome of the revenue system is still regressive.

Sources of revenue, 2000

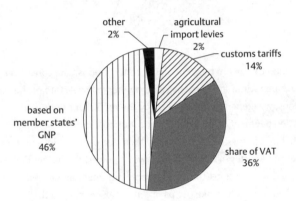

Net contributions

For Spain, Portugal, Greece, and Ireland the revenue contributions have been far outweighed by their receipts from the cohesion and agricultural policies. For Britain, where incomes per head are also below the EU average, this is far from being the case. Because of the small farm sector, British receipts from the CAP are relatively low; and Britain contributed more than the others in import levies. Despite the rebate that was obtained to offset this special disadvantage, Britain's net contribution to the budget remained in the 1990s around 0.3 per cent of GDP. Apart from Germany which, as a rich country gaining much from

States' net budgetary payments or receipts
(percentage of GDP, average 1992–9, minus sign net payments)

Belgium	−0.31
Denmark	0.20
Germany	−0.67
Greece	4.45
Spain	1.07
France	−0.12
Ireland	5.15
Italy	−0.12
Netherlands	−0.60
Austria (1995–7)	−0.34
Portugal	3.06
Finland (1995–7)	−0.03
Sweden (1995–7)	−0.49
United Kingdom	−0.30

(Source: *Financing the European Union*, October 1998, Annex 8, table 5)

the Community, willingly accepted for many years its role as the largest net contributor, the other states were until the 1990s all net recipients. But the Germans, with their average incomes reduced and their own budget burdened by the entry of the former GDR into the Federal Republic, became increasingly reluctant to bear this burden too; the net contribution of the Dutch has joined that of the Germans at over 0.6 per cent of GDP; those of the Swedes, Austrians, and Belgians were in the 1990s, like that of the British, in the range of 0.3–0.5 per cent, with the French and Italians around 0.1 per cent of GDP. Resistance to high net contributions has become normal, rather than being seen as an example of the British lack of European solidarity. While this may cause wry amusement on this side of the Channel, it is a dangerous development. For the Union will need to maintain solidarity, and in particular to be ready to allocate resources to assist the integration of Central and East Europeans, if it is to continue to provide a framework for peace and prosperity after the forthcoming enlargement. Further budgetary reform will surely be necessary.

It is not likely that the British rebate can continue in its present form beyond the enlargement. Although the government has in the past made clear that it would regard any such change as justifying a veto, it has to take into account that net contributions already bear more heavily on Germany, the Netherlands, Sweden, and Austria than on the UK. Some *ad hoc* solutions have been devised for burden-sharing; and the Berlin European Council decided to reduce by three-quarters the shares that those four pay towards financing the British rebate. But in order to avoid future conflicts, a more equitable system is not only a British but also a general interest. The Commission suggested, in *Agenda 2000*, that the rebate could become part of what it called a 'generalized system of corrections', casting the net wider in correcting the anomalies.

Such a reform is hard to achieve. In 1988 Italy, where incomes per head had recently surpassed the EC average, prevented the adoption of a new revenue resource that would have required the richer to pay more than the poorer. In 1999, when the European Council decided on the financial perspective for 2000–6, France and Spain succeeded in limiting some of the changes in the agricultural and cohesion budgets, which would have reduced their privileges in order to release resources to help pay for the forthcoming enlargement; and Britain refused to accept reduction of its rebate though others have proportionately higher net contributions. Governments, looking over their shoulders at domestic public opinion, are naturally reluctant to renounce their privileged positions. But previous decisions on major budgetary packages have shown that reform is possible.

The ceiling of 1.27 per cent of GNP gives enough scope for what the Union has to do at present. But we cannot be at all sure that this will continue to be so. The financial perspective sets the limit for expenditure of an EU with twenty-one member states at €103.5 billion in 2006, or 1.09 per cent of the enlarged Union's estimated GNP. This may fall well short of what the Union will need for all it will have to do, for example in helping Central and East Europeans to perform well enough within the Union, or in discharging its growing responsibilities for foreign policy and security. Given such challenges, the ceiling of 1.27 per cent may not be enough, let alone the provision in the financial perspective. It is not too soon to give thought to the possible implications for budgetary reform.

Chapter 6
Social policy,
environmental policy

The EU has been given some of its powers, such as those to establish the single market, because its size offers advantages that are beyond the reach of the individual member states. Other powers are designed to prevent member states from damaging each other. The environment is one field in which powers have been given to that end, with general agreement that it is desirable. Another is social policy, where there has been sharp disagreement as to how far EU intervention is required.

Social policy

The term social policy has a narrower meaning in EU parlance than it generally has in Britain. It does not refer to the range of policies, including health, housing, and social services, with which the welfare state is concerned. The pattern of such services differs from country to country, reflecting their political and social cultures; and it is widely accepted that the cross-border effects of the differences are not sufficient to justify intervention by the Union. In the Treaty and EU jargon, however, social policy concerns matters relating to employment, where there are also wide variations from country to country. But since conditions of employment touch more closely on the single market, there has been pressure to harmonize member states' policies in order to prevent employees in states with higher standards suffering as a result of competition from those with lower standards.

The first such example was the article on equal pay in the Treaty of Rome. France was ahead of other founder states in having legislated that women be paid equally with men for equal work. In order to keep sectors that employed a high proportion of women competitive, France demanded that its partners introduce equal pay too. With the general movement towards gender equality, this was to become one of the most popular European laws. By the time of the Amsterdam Treaty, there was ready agreement to extend the principle from equal pay to equal opportunities and equal treatment in all matters relating to employment.

The Single European Act extended the scope of social policy in two directions: providing for legislation on health and safety at work and for the encouragement of dialogue between representatives of management and labour at European level. While Mrs Thatcher had fought hard against the influence of 'corporatist' relationships in Britain, she doubtless reckoned that such dialogue at European level would not be of much consequence; and the case against undercutting standards of health and safety was generally agreed. So although Community social policy was to become one of Thatcher's bêtes noires, she accepted these provisions of the Single Act as part of the package that included the single market programme.

In 1989 Delors, who saw higher standards of social legislation as being, for workers, a necessary counterpart to the single market, proposed a Social Charter that was approved by all but one in the European Council. Thatcher dissented. Although she accepted some of its provisions, such as free movement for workers and the right to join (or not) a trade union, she contested others such as a right for workers to participate in companies' decision-taking, as well as maximum working hours – which, much to the British government's disgust, were subsequently enacted by a qualified majority vote under the treaty article on health and safety at work. Major followed her example when he secured

Britain's opt-out from the provisions on social policy in the Maastricht Treaty, which therefore appeared in a protocol that applied to all the other member states. It was only after Labour's election victory in 1997 that there was unanimous agreement to convert the protocol into a social chapter in the Amsterdam Treaty; and it was accompanied by a new chapter aimed at achieving 'a high level of employment and of social protection'. But Blair has continued to promote the cause of flexible labour markets.

Social policy

Social policy in the EU jargon means policy relating to labour relations. It was the subject of a Protocol to the Maastricht Treaty, signed by all the member states save the UK, because the then British government did not accept it. The Labour government elected in May 1997, however, accepted it as a section of the Amsterdam Treaty.

EU social policy focuses on several areas: improvement of the working environment to protect workers' health and safety; working conditions; information and consultation of workers; equality between men and women at work; integration of people excluded from the labour market. This is done by supporting and coordinating national policies and by legislation, enacted in certain areas by co-decision between Council and Parliament. The Commission is required to encourage co-operation among member states in matters such as training, social security, accident prevention.

Amsterdam also authorized the Council to take action to combat discrimination 'based on sex, racial or ethnic origin, religion or belief, age or sexual orientation'.

'Anglo-Saxons' and 'Rhinelanders'

Blair has emphasized deregulation and flexibility in his approach to the EU, on the grounds that it will make the European economy more competitive and increase employment. While labour markets are not the only sector of the economy in which deregulation is advocated, they are seen as among the most important.

While this British approach has been called 'Anglo-Saxon' because of similarities with American economic philosophy, the alternative has become known as the 'Rhineland' approach, with Germany the leading example. There the emphasis in labour markets has been on solidarity and social protection rather than flexibility. Much of the regulation to achieve this has been negotiated between employers and unions, called in Germany the social partners. This has reflected a culture of consensus in civil society in reaction against the ways of the preceding totalitarian dictatorship; and it has built on long-standing traditions of solidarity, such as the acceptance of responsibility in the private sector for the high standards of technical training. The results have included the outstanding economic success of the post-war decades and the continuing strength of German exports. But although the burden of integrating the eastern Länder into the German economy is one cause of the less successful performance in the 1990s, Germany is also criticized for reluctance to introduce more flexibility into the labour market and to reform industrial and financial organization and the tax system, in response to current developments in the global economy.

The Rhine also flows through the Netherlands; and the Dutch too have a highly consensual economic and political system. Faced with critical economic problems in the 1980s, they began a process of reform which led to what is called the 'Polder model', introducing market-oriented reforms into what remains a consensual system; and they have achieved lower unemployment, higher efficiency, and a good all-round economic performance. Scandinavians have much in common with this approach.

Employment policy

The Amsterdam Treaty introduced a new section on employment in response to concern about the high level of unemployment in the EU. Its main purpose is to encourage co-operation among the member states with respect to their employment policies.

The member states provide annual reports on their employment policies to the Council and Commission, which draw up a report for the European Council. Guidelines are then issued to the states to be taken into account in their employment policies; and the Council can make recommendations to governments. The Council, in co-decision with the Parliament, may decide to spend money from the budget to encourage exchanges of information and best practices, provide comparative analysis and advice, promote innovative approaches, and fund pilot projects.

This has raised the profile of employment policy in the Union but it remains to be seen how much effect it has on governments' policies.

The French, while stressing social protection, rely more on government leadership and regulation; and they too, despite criticism that they are slow to reform, have performed well through the 1990s on most measures save their high rate of unemployment, which remained above 10 per cent throughout the decade.

It is often forgotten that the British, for more than three decades after World War Two, had an economy that was highly regulated by both collective bargaining and government intervention. It was in reaction against this that the reforms of the Thatcher period moved Britain sharply towards the Anglo-Saxon model. While the intention of Blair's 'third way' is to prevent such oscillation by occupying a centre ground in between, much of the emphasis on economic flexibility and his government's enterprise-friendly orientation derives from his predecessors' reforms, as well as from an older British tradition of economic liberalism.

The improved British economic performance in the 1990s has helped to give credibility to the Anglo-Saxon approach, as has the dynamism of the Irish economy. But most important has been the sustained success of the American economy, with its low unemployment and high growth, from which the conclusion may be drawn that flexibility suits the new wave of technological development. While the degree of laissez-faire in the American approach to social policy is resisted, a certain consensus may be emerging in the EU that methods such as bench-marking and peer pressure are more suitable than social legislation for reducing unemployment, as well as for some measures to create a dynamic and competitive economy. In so far as this is so, the period of conflict about social policy between Britain and the rest may be drawing to a close.

Environmental policy

Polluted air and water cannot be prevented from moving out of one state and causing damage in another. So there is an interest in common standards to control the pollution at its source. The same applies to the environmental effects of goods traded in the single market. The Single European Act provided for a Community environmental policy to deal with these problems. It also affirmed that the EC's objective was to 'preserve, protect and improve the quality of the environment'.

Over 200 environmental measures have been enacted, responding to a wide range of environmental concerns: air and water pollution; waste disposal; noise limits for aircraft and motor vehicles; wildlife habitats; quality standards for drinking and bathing water. In 1988 a law was passed to reduce the incidence of acid rain, cutting emissions of sulphur dioxide and nitrogen oxides by 58 per cent by stages over the next fifteen years. Standards of protection against dangerous chemicals were raised following the entry of the environmentally conscious Swedes into the Union.

While EU legislation has always allowed member states to set their own higher standards in other matters, Scandinavian pressure led to an article in the Amsterdam Treaty allowing states to have higher standards for traded products too, provided they can persuade the Commission that these are not protectionist devices. But given the extent of the environmental legislation, there have been remarkably few complaints about it. A requirement that member states conduct environmental impact assessments before acting in ways likely to cause damage did get in the way of plans for a road by-passing Winchester, in the south of England, on the grounds that the assessment had not been properly carried out; and the British government saw this as meddling in local affairs. But such complaints are rather rare. The environmental policy came at a time when Europeans were rapidly becoming greener, so it became one of the Community's most popular policies, as the provision for equal pay had done before; and like policy for gender equality it was strengthened by the Amsterdam Treaty, which required that 'environmental protection requirements' must be integrated into other Community policies, 'with a view to promoting sustainable development'. It was then agreed to prepare plans to integrate environmental concerns into EU policies for sectors such as agriculture, energy, and transport, which taken together could amount to a strategy for sustainable development.

As we saw in Chapter 5, agreement seems harder to reach on taxation than on legislation. The Commission has proposed a carbon and energy tax to discourage damaging emissions of carbon dioxide (CO_2). But this was opposed by industrial sectors that use a lot of energy, arguing that it would make them uncompetitive unless other industrialized countries too adopted the tax. There was also opposition on grounds of fiscal sovereignty. So nothing has come of it so far. But the international dimension of the Union's environmental policy has fared better.

The Union has made a substantial impact on international action regarding climate change. In 1986, when it had become evident that chlorofluorocarbons (CFCs) could destroy the ozone layer and thus endanger life on earth, the EC succeeded in breaking a deadlock in negotiations for an agreement, which has since done much to stem the degradation. Then in 1997 the Union played the central part in the negotiations in Kyoto for an agreement to stem the emissions of CO_2 and other greenhouse gases, which appear to be leading to a very dangerous degree of global warming. Despite American reluctance to accept anything like adequate targets, or to respond to the demands of Third World countries for assistance in the necessary technological adaptations as a condition for their participation, the EU ensured that there was a significant outcome. But the EU itself may have difficulty in meeting its not very ambitious target of a reduction of 8 per cent in emissions of three principal gases by 2010. The only legal obligation of member states is to produce national programmes to reduce their emissions; and a stronger system is likely to be necessary if even that target is to be hit.

The Union also faces a very big task in ensuring that prospective member states from Central and Eastern Europe, grossly polluted during the Soviet period, measure up to its environmental standards. The temptation will be to seek very long transitional periods before the newcomers are required to apply all the EU laws, and to keep some protection against unfair competition from those that are exonerated from costly obligations in the mean time. Adequate assistance to bring them up to scratch would be a better solution.

Chapter 7
'An area of freedom, security and justice'

Ernest Bevin, the great Foreign Secretary in the first post-war Labour government, said that the aim of his foreign policy 'really was . . . to grapple with the whole problem of passports and visas', so that he could 'go down to Victoria Station', where trains departed for the Continent, 'get a railway ticket, and go where the Hell I liked without a passport or anything else'. The old trade unionist retained his vision of the brotherhood of man. But the foreign minister found himself defending the sovereignty of states; and he rejected the idea of British membership of the emergent Community, which was eventually to make the realization of his vision feasible.

Already in 1958 the Rome Treaty included 'persons', along with goods, services, and capital, in the four freedoms of movement across the frontiers between the member states. For 'persons' this was limited to the right to cross them for purposes of work. A quarter of a century later, the Single European Act defined the internal market as 'an area without internal frontiers'. Mrs Thatcher's government held that these words implied no change, because they were qualified by the addition 'in accordance with the Treaty', which in relevant respects still stood. But governments of the more federalist states intended to take the words literally: to abolish controls at their mutual borders and thus make movement across them free for all.

This idea was given legal expression in the Schengen Agreements of 1985 and 1990, Schengen being the small town in Luxembourg, symbolically alongside the frontiers with both France and Germany, where these three states, together with Belgium and the Netherlands, signed the agreements. The number of signatories has since grown until what is often called Schengenland includes all the EU states save Britain and Ireland, while Denmark has an ambiguous relationship.

Schengen had two main aims. The first concerned border controls: to eliminate those internal to Schengenland; establish controls round its external frontier; and set rules to deal with asylum, immigration, and the movement or residence of other countries' nationals within the area. The second was to co-operate in combating crime.

Cross-border criminal activity grows for reasons similar to those that drive cross-border economic activity: advancing technology, particularly in transport and communications. As with trade, cross-border co-operation is needed if the rule of law is to keep abreast of it. With the intense relationship engendered by their economic integration, the member states have a special need for such co-operation. A first step was taken in 1974 with the 'Trevi' agreement to exchange information about terrorism; and the ministers and officials involved soon found it useful to include other forms of crime. This was a precursor of Schengen, which forged closer co-operation among law enforcement agencies of the states that were ready to go farther together, and which has led, in the fifteen years since the first Schengen Agreement, to an 'acquis' of over 3,000 pages of legal texts, applying to the big majority of EU member states.

Maastricht and the third pillar

Cross-border aspects of crime and the movement of people affect all member states, not just those of Schengenland. It was agreed that the Maaastricht Treaty should provide for co-operation in these fields.

Terrorism, drugs, fraud, and 'other serious forms of crime' were listed in the Treaty, along with external border controls, asylum, immigration, and movement across the internal borders by nationals from states outside the Union. The member states' judicial, administrative, police, and customs authorities were to co-operate in order to deal with them.

Some states, such as Germany, wanted this to be done within the Community institutions, with the Commission, Court, and Parliament as well as the Council playing their normal parts. Others such as Britain, defending their sovereignty, wanted to exclude as far as possible the institutions other than the Council. The upshot was the new 'third pillar' for Co-operation in Justice and Home Affairs (CJHA), set up alongside the Community 'first pillar'. The institutions for the CJHA were intergovernmental, with the unanimity procedure in the Council, only consultative roles for the Parliament and Commission, and none at all for the Court. The policy instruments were to be joint positions and actions determined by the Council, and conventions ratified by all the member states. One of the conventions was to establish the new policing body, Europol.

Not surprisingly, given the requirement of unanimous agreement among the fifteen governments before a decision could be taken, there had not been much progress by the time the Amsterdam Treaty was negotiated. No convention had yet entered into force and action in other respects was slow. But concern about cross-border crime and illegal immigration continued to grow; and the Eastern enlargement, expected to bring new problems, was approaching. So most member states wanted a stronger system.

Amsterdam and the first pillar too

The Amsterdam Treaty affirmed the intention to establish what it rather grandly called 'an area of freedom, security and justice' (AFSJ). While conditions in the Union are, in a general sense, notably free, secure, and just when compared with almost all other parts of the world, the words are used in the treaty in a more specific sense: freedom refers to free movement across internal borders; security, to protection against cross-border crime; and justice, mainly to judicial co-operation in civil as well as criminal matters. It remains to be seen whether it was wise to appropriate words that have such wide and noble significance for such particular ends. The answer may depend on how far and how soon they will be achieved.

As regards *freedom* of movement, almost all the Schengen acquis has already been transferred from the third to the first pillar. Thus the right of people to move freely throughout Schengenland is guaranteed by the Community institutions, though some member states have had to restore border checks temporarily in order to deal with influxes from other member states of non-EU nationals with false visas. As this shows, the external border controls are not yet satisfactory. Nor is the common policy on immigration and asylum complete. Nor will there be freedom of movement without border checks throughout the Union while Britain, Denmark, and Ireland retain their controls.

The removal of border controls within Schengenland is nevertheless a major achievement, as is the transfer of these competences to the Community, with the Court of Justice fulfilling its normal functions – except in the fields of internal security and law and order, which remain under the control of the member states. For the five years following the treaty's entry into force, that is until May 2004, the Community institutions are to operate in a largely intergovernmental mode, with Council unanimity, consultation with the Parliament, and the Com-mission sharing its right to initiate legislation with the member states. But at the end of the five years, qualified majority voting, co-decision, and the Commission's sole right of initiative are to apply, provided that the Schengenland governments agree to this move, by qualified majority for some elements but unanimously for others, which they are quite likely to do if things are going well, otherwise perhaps not.

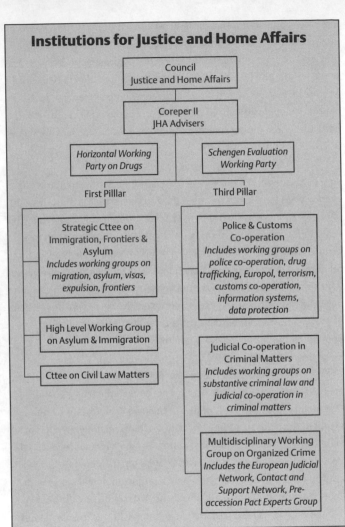

Institutions for Justice and Home Affairs

Council
Justice and Home Affairs

Coreper II
JHA Advisers

Horizontal Working Party on Drugs

Schengen Evaluation Working Party

First Pilllar

Third Pillar

Strategic Cttee on Immigration, Frontiers & Asylum
Includes working groups on migration, asylum, visas, expulsion, frontiers

Police & Customs Co-operation
Includes working groups on police co-operation, drug trafficking, Europol, terrorism, customs co-operation, information systems, data protection

High Level Working Group on Asylum & Immigration

Cttee on Civil Law Matters

Judicial Co-operation in Criminal Matters
Includes working groups on substantive criminal law and judicial co-operation in criminal matters

Multidisciplinary Working Group on Organized Crime
Includes the European Judicial Network, Contact and Support Network, Pre-accession Pact Experts Group

The European Union

Determined to keep its border controls, Britain opted out of the Amsterdam Treaty's provisions on freedom of movement; and Ireland, enjoying open frontiers with the UK, had to do the same. But both have the right to opt into specific measures, provided the other governments agree unanimously in each case. The British government has indicated it intends to participate fully in the Schengen acquis, apart from the aspects relating to border controls, for which it awaits evidence that the external border controls and internal co-operation are sufficiently effective. Denmark, which had signed up to the Schengen Agreements, has nevertheless opted out of their transfer into the Community, with consequences that are hard to predict.

As regards *security*, the fight against cross-border crime remains mainly in the intergovernmental third pillar, whose designation, since competence regarding free movement has been transferred to the Community, has been reduced to 'Police and Judicial Co-operation in Criminal Matters'. In line with ever-growing concern about crime, the Amsterdam Treaty extended the list to include trafficking in persons, offences against children, and corruption; and money-laundering, forging money, and 'cyber-crime' have been added since.

Police co-operation has developed significantly, resulting for example in big seizures of drugs on their way to Britain. Europol has made a useful contribution, though it could not become fully operational until its convention was fully ratified by all member states in July 1999, over five years after the Maastricht Treaty had provided for it. While the third pillar remains predominantly intergovernmental, with the unanimity procedure prevailing in the Council, the Amsterdam Treaty did provide that conventions, when ratified by half the member states, would enter into force in those states. There is also a role for the Court of Justice, which was given authority to rule on the interpretation of Union laws and on disputes between member states or between them and the Commission.

In order to give free movement and the fight against crime a lift in the Union's political priorities, the European Council held a special meeting on the subject at Tampere under Finnish Presidency in October 1999. It decided among other things to establish a high-level European Police College and a body called Eurojust, bringing together member states' prosecutors, magistrates, and police officers to co-operate in criminal investigation and prosecution.

In the narrow definition of *justice* as judicial co-operation, some specific steps have been taken for member states to assist each other in cross-border problems relating to the recognition and enforcement of judgments, though not much has been done about the rights of victims of crime. Not satisfied with this, France proposed a 'European judicial area' to work towards harmonization of member states' laws regarding cross-border litigation and enforcement of judgments, together with common minimum standards in citizens' access to courts. Britain preferred the idea of mutual recognition among the member states, after the pattern of mutual recognition of rules in the single market; and this was accepted at the European Council in Tampere. But proposals for harmonization are not likely to go away.

In a broader definition of the word, distributive justice has been an issue in this field since Germany, with a much larger number of asylum-seekers than other member states, wanted measures to share the cost. This was resisted by other states, though Britain, where in 1999 the pressure of asylum-seekers almost reached the German level, became more sympathetic. With others likewise affected, the EU allocated a modest sum in 1999 to help with the cost of refugees: a small step in the direction of burden-sharing.

In a yet broader sense of justice, the Amsterdam Treaty responded to criticism that the Union had emphasized restrictions on immigration and asylum at the expense of concern about the treatment of the human beings involved. In the face of widespread public backlash against them, the treaty provided for measures to safeguard their rights, together with action more generally to combat racism and xenophobia. It remains to be seen how much will be done.

What's in the name?

Freedom of movement within Schengenland is an almost complete reality. If Bevin were able to go to the Gare du Nord or the Gare de Lyon today, he could buy a ticket and go without a passport wherever he liked within Schengenland, though not, unfortunately, to Victoria Station.

It is far from certain, however, that police and judicial co-operation under the third pillar will deliver enough security from cross-border crime. The Community pillar has the competence to act in this field, but until 2004 it too is subject mainly to unanimity; and the effort is concentrated in the third pillar where that procedure prevails. Such crime continues to proliferate and it is doubtful whether the EU institutions as they stand at present are strong enough to win the battle against it. Judicial co-operation is good as far as it goes. But, again owing to institutional weaknesses, it does not yet go far enough.

Nor should it be forgotten that the absence of Britain, and hence of Ireland too, from full participation in this aspect of the Community pillar weakens the Union, and is probably storing up trouble for Britain itself. The opt-out is the main reason why responsibility for matters that belong together is divided between the first and third pillars, impeding action and making something that is already hard enough for citizens to grasp yet more incomprehensible. It is also another example of British failure to participate in a Community project which, in all likelihood, Britain will sooner or later decide to join after most of the decisions have been taken by others.

It is to be hoped that, despite these problems, the Area of Freedom,

Security and Justice will be a success in its own terms. But it remains questionable whether the name is well chosen. For the meaning of the words in their proper sense is a great deal more profound, and in this sense the Union has much of which it can be proud. It seems a pity to use the term in the narrow sense where, at least over the medium term, full success is not assured.

Chapter 8

A great civilian power . . . and more, or less?

The main motives for creating the Community were peace between France, Germany, and the other member states, and prosperity for their citizens. But while their mutual relationship was particularly intense, relations with their neighbours and with countries further afield were also important; and the logic of subsidiarity, that the Community should have responsibility for what it can do better than the member states acting separately, began to be applied to external as well as internal affairs.

The Community's external relations were, in line with its powers, originally concentrated in the economic field. But there were from the outset also political aims. For Germany, bordering on the Soviet bloc and with East Germany under Soviet control, the priority was solidarity in resistance to Soviet pressure. The French had a broader vision of the Community as a power in the world. Relations with the United States were a central element: for Monnet, in the form of a partnership between the Community and the USA; for de Gaulle, to defy American hegemony. Monnet's view was widely shared and the Community came to be seen as a potential 'great civilian power'.

Many in France went beyond this, envisaging a Europe that could challenge American dominance in the field of defence. In other countries this view was generally resisted. But co-operation in foreign policy evolved to the point where it was given the name 'Common Foreign and Security Policy'; and Britain, which had long been adamantly opposed to common action by the EU on defence, in 1999 joined France in initiating a modest EU defence capacity. But this is still a minor element in the Union's external relations. The Community's external economic policies remain much more important.

External economic relations

The Rome Treaty gave the Community its common external tariff as an instrument for trade policy, called in the jargon 'common commercial policy'. This was not a foregone conclusion. Some wanted the member states to keep their existing tariffs, below the average in Germany and Benelux, higher in France and Italy. But the French insisted on the common tariff, partly because they feared competition from cheap imports seeping through the low-tariff states, but partly also because they wanted the Community to have an instrument with which it could start to become a force in world affairs.

This has remained a persistent French theme. It was one of the motives for the drive towards the single currency, challenging the hegemony of the dollar; and it has continued with the effort to build a European defence capacity, for which the term 'Europe puissance' has been coined, contrasted with a mere European 'space' preoccupied with business affairs. Neither those French who were highly protectionist, nor the British who at that time criticized the common tariff as a protectionist device, envisaged that it would in fact be the trigger for the Kennedy round of tariff cuts, which was the first step towards the Community's role as the foremost promoter of world trade liberalization, and thus also towards demonstrating the power of a common instrument of external policy.

That power has been shown in the field of agriculture too, with less fortunate results. The system of import levies and export subsidies has

Shares of world trade of EU, USA, Japan, and others, 1997

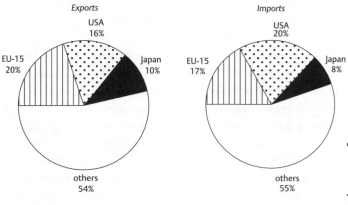

Exports

USA 16%
EU-15 20%
Japan 10%
others 54%

Imports

USA 20%
EU-15 17%
Japan 8%
others 55%

been used in a highly protectionist way, to the detriment of the Community's consumers and international trade relations, including its own industrial exports. But the external trade policy, taken as a whole, has been of considerable benefit both to its citizens and to international trade.

The same can be said of another major instrument of external economic policy: development aid, which, likewise on French insistence, started with the Rome Treaty's provision for a fund for the then colonies of member states. This has since burgeoned so that the Union provides aid for countries throughout the Third World. In the 1990s, the capacity to provide assistance was applied to a different purpose: to help the transformation of Central and East European countries from Soviet-style centralization towards market economies and pluralist democracies, as well as that of Russia and other Soviet Union successor states.

Thus the EU, together with its member states, has become by far the world's largest source of aid; and in Europe the Union's instruments of trade and aid policy, together with the prospect of membership for most of the Central and East European countries, have been the major external influence favouring their successful transformation. It was indeed fortunate that France insisted on the original grant of instruments for the Community's external policy.

External trade relations are conducted effectively by the Community institutions. Policies are decided and trade agreements approved by the Council under the procedure of qualified majority; negotiations are conducted by the Commission within the policy mandate thus decided, and in consultation with a special committee appointed by the Council; and the Court has jurisdiction on points of law. Parliaments do not usually play much part in relation to trade negotiations, apart from formally approving the results. But the Treaty does not even provide for consultation of the European Parliament about matters of trade policy, though it is accorded the right to give or withhold its assent over treaties of association and, more importantly, of accession. The Parliament does, moreover, play a significant part in external relations in, for example, the joint committees of MEPs with parliamentarians of states with Europe or Partnership Agreements, and interparliamentary delegations to other partners such as the USA, Japan, Australia, Canada, and New Zealand; it has been addressed by many Heads of State, including Presidents Reagan, Havel, and Sadat, and by Pope John Paul II; and it is consulted on the Common Foreign and Security Policy.

When the Rome Treaty was drafted, trade in goods was all-important; trade in services was of little account, and was not mentioned in the chapter on the common commercial policy. But services by now comprise about one-third of all world trade. Yet despite the success of the normal Community system as it applies to the trade in goods, trade in services has remained subject to more intergovernmental procedures. While the momentum of successful negotiations on trade in goods has carried the Community through a series of trade rounds,

15. The world's temporal and spiritual powers address the
Parliament: Ronald Reagan and Pope John Paul II.

these procedures could still weaken its capacity to negotiate effectively
on services. So the Nice Treaty applies qualified majority voting to
trade in all services save in the fields of culture, audio-visual services,
education, health and social services, and some transport services.

The environment too has become a major field for international
negotiation; and though the Community's external policy remains
subject to a more intergovernmental procedure than its trade policy,
the EU has none the less made a significant impact on negotiations to
counter global warming and destruction of the ozone layer.

Despite the introduction of the euro, the EU does not yet show signs of
playing a similar part in the international monetary system. It is early
days yet but, as is argued in Chapter 10, the institutional arrangements
for conducting an external monetary policy are not at present strong
enough to make a positive European contribution likely in this field.

Foreign policy

Co-operation in foreign policy among the member states was introduced in 1970 as an element of deepening along with the widening to include Britain, Ireland, and Denmark. The name given to this activity was European Political Co-operation (EPC): the word 'political' being used by ministries of foreign affairs, distinguishing what they saw as 'high politics' from such matters as economics, evidently regarded as low. But the Community's external economic policies were already a great deal more important than anything the EPC was to achieve during the following years, particularly as France, in the early years after de Gaulle, insisted that the EPC be kept not only intergovernmental but also rigorously separate from the Community.

The EPC did achieve at least one important early result when the member states got human rights placed on the agenda of the Conference on Security and Co-operation in Europe. The Soviet Union surprisingly accepted the text that was finally adopted; and though nobody then thought this of much consequence, it gave support to the agitation that finally contributed to the dissolution of the Soviet bloc. More generally, the member states' diplomats developed ways of working together that were to produce many joint positions on a wide range of subjects, both in relations with other states and in the United Nations. By 1985 France was ready to accept that the EPC should come closer to the Community and it was included in the Single European Act.

The next formal development of foreign policy co-operation was its incorporation in the Maastricht Treaty alongside the Community, as the 'second pillar' of the EU. The prospect of German unification had alarmed the French, who feared that the larger Germany would downgrade the Franco-German partnership and pursue an autonomous eastern policy. Just as they promoted the single currency to anchor Germany in the Community, so they wanted a common foreign policy to limit German autonomy in relations with the East. The Germans, far from opposing this, saw it as part of the design for a Europe united on federal lines. So in 1990 President Mitterrand and Chancellor Kohl proposed the IGC on 'political union' to run in parallel with the one on economic and monetary union.

When Mrs Thatcher asked them what they meant by political union, she got no clear answer. One reason was that, while both were agreed on the idea of a common foreign policy, which was one of the two specific things to which the term was applied, they disagreed about reform of the institutions, which was the other. For while the French wanted to strengthen the intergovernmental elements, in particular the European Council, the Germans wanted to move towards a federal system by strengthening the Parliament. So they could hardly speak with one voice about it. Thatcher wanted neither and, though she accepted the existing EPC, did not want the Community institutions to have a hand in it. While Germany did envisage that foreign policy would move towards becoming a Community competence, France too opposed the idea; and the outcome was the intergovernmental 'second pillar' for a Common Foreign and Security Policy (CFSP).

The CFSP was given a grander name than the EPC and more elaborate institutions. Following Europe's poor showing in the Gulf War, defence was mentioned in the treaty, but in ambiguous terms to accommodate both the French desire for an autonomous European defence capacity and British opposition to any such thing, for fear it could weaken Nato. So nothing much resulted from the use of the word defence. Nor indeed did the CFSP produce notably better results than the EPC had done before. So there was a second try, in the 1996 IGC, to devise a satisfactory second pillar.

The treaty sets very general objectives for the CFSP, ranging from international co-operation to support for democracy, the rule of law, and human rights. In an attempt to make the Union more decisive, there is provision for voting by qualified majority. But this is hedged about by rights of opting out and veto. Thus there can be QMV on common positions and joint actions, but only if taken 'on the basis of a common strategy', which has to be adopted unanimously; and that can narrow the scope for decisions taken by QMV as much as a member state government may desire. Governments can also refer decisions they oppose to the European Council, where again they can apply the veto; and they can opt out of decisions when they wish to do so.

This complexity reflects the reality that where actions depend on the instruments that belong to member states, not the Union, they are likely to be applied with varying degrees of commitment, to put it mildly, by governments that have serious objections. But a majority decision to act will be properly applied if it depends on the use of an instrument that belongs to the Union. Such instruments can be fiscal, such as the common external tariff, or financial, such as aid and assistance, or monetary, such as the euro; and the Union does dispose of these. An instrument can also be a legal act; and in external relations association agreements are examples where QMV does not up to now apply. The Union will also, with the rapid deployment force, dispose of instruments in the field of defence. But sending soldiers on missions where they may be killed is seen as too sensitive a matter to be decided by the Union against the wishes of the state of which they are citizens. So majority voting is excluded from the field of defence. But apart from this, the limits to how far QMV can be of practical use, without opting out or unanimity in the background, are set by the extent to which the Union is given common instruments that can be used to carry out the decisions.

It remains to be seen how far this attempt to insert more majority voting into the CFSP can lead to more decisive common action. One of the other changes introduced by the Amsterdam Treaty has, however, begun to have an impact: the appointment of a 'High Representative', who is at the same time Secretary-General of the Council Secretariat, to 'assist' the Council's President-in-Office in representing the Union in the field of CFSP. Javier Solana was given this position, and also that of Secretary-General of Western European Union (WEU). Combining these three posts, and with his track record as a successful Secretary-General of Nato, he is well placed to influence the intergovernmental decisions of the CFSP.

It is, however, the Community institutions that control the instruments of external economic policy; and here Christopher Patten has the central role, as Commissioner with overall responsibility in this field, along with Commissioners Pascal Lamy, who is responsible for trade policy, Poul Nielson for most of the development aid, and Gunter Verheugen for the accession negotiations. The part that the treaty gives the Commission

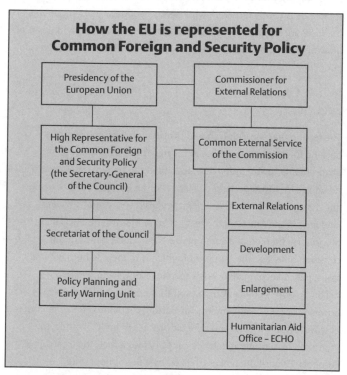

How the EU is represented for Common Foreign and Security Policy

- Presidency of the European Union
- Commissioner for External Relations
- High Representative for the Common Foreign and Security Policy (the Secretary-General of the Council)
- Common External Service of the Commission
- Secretariat of the Council
  - External Relations
  - Development
  - Enlargement
  - Humanitarian Aid Office – ECHO
- Policy Planning and Early Warning Unit

to play in the making of common foreign and security policy, of merely submitting proposals when requested by the Council to do so, fails to recognize this reality.

A policy planning unit was also established in the Council Secretariat, drawing staff from the Secretariat itself, the member states, WEU, and the Commission, to prepare thinking on CFSP issues likely to arise. The Parliament too became involved in the foreign policy process through the inclusion of CFSP expenditure in the part of the Community budget over which it shares control with the Council. But this does not apply for military or defence operations or 'where the Council unanimously decides otherwise'. The defect of these arrangements is that substantial sums of money for CFSP purposes can, as crises in the Balkans have shown, be urgently required, whereas the budgetary arrangements for the CFSP are not adapted to putting up such money fast; and this is a grievous defect, because while such funds are awaited crises can spin out of control.

Security

The feeling that the Union should provide more effective military backing for its common policy in former Yugoslavia spurred governments to strengthen its capacity in the field of defence. While all recognize that they depend on Nato and the USA for defence against any major threat to their security, they used somewhat stronger language in the Amsterdam Treaty than at Maastricht, envisaging 'the progressive framing of a common defence policy, which might lead to a common defence', the purpose of which is to include humanitarian tasks, peace-keeping, and 'crisis management, including peace-making'. More significant than aspirations expressed in the treaties, however, are the arrangements for putting them into effect; and instead of leaving it to the slow and difficult process of an IGC to turn the aspiration of a common defence capacity into a fact, the treaty gave the European Council the power to do so by a unanimous vote.

The war over Kosovo then demonstrated that Europeans, though their defence expenditure amounted to two-thirds that of the Americans, were capable of delivering only one-tenth of the firepower; and their influence over the conduct of the action was correspondingly limited. This brought together the British and French, who had made the principal European contribution, to launch their defence initiative. Experience in the Gulf and the Balkan wars had shown the French that they had to come closer to Nato if they were to make an effective military contribution. The British for their part had come to see the merit of working with the French; and, having declined to become a founder member of the euro-zone, the government saw defence as a field in which a central role for Britain in the Union could be secured.

The result was the joint proposal for an EU rapid reaction force 'up to' 50,000–60,000 strong, which was adopted by the European Council in Helsinki in December 1999; and it was agreed to integrate WEU into the Union. The Union can use WEU's military capacities and has established its own defence planning and staff structure, with Council meetings in which defence ministers participate along with the foreign ministers, a Military Committee representing member states' 'defence chiefs', and military staff within the Council Secretariat. The rapid reaction force is to be created by 2003, to undertake peace-keeping and crisis-management autonomously 'where Nato as a whole is not engaged', though Nato, which in practice means American, facilities such as air transport and satellite-based intelligence will usually be required; and this means American consent to any substantial operations. Thus the British government's fears about weakening Nato have been allayed; and all member states, including Austria, Finland, Ireland, and Sweden, with their traditions of neutrality, are reassured by the provisions that any member state can opt out of, or into, any action.

This illustrates the difficulties confronting the Union's defence capacity. A critical mass of member states must agree to an action before it can be undertaken; for substantial operations that require Nato facilities and hence American consent, the Americans may not agree to what Europeans want to do, which would give rise to tensions within Nato; and where a European critical mass and American agreement are both available, the intergovernmental arrangements may be too weak to devise and manage a successful operation. While Nato's system is also intergovernmental, American hegemonial leadership has caused it to work. There is no hegemon among the member states; and while this makes it possible to develop the Union as a working democracy, it will at the same time make an intergovernmental system in the field of defence hard to operate. The present arrangements may, however, become a step towards further reforms that will surely be required to make the system effective.

While such reforms are likely to introduce more federal elements into the institutional structure responsible for the Union's defence operations, they should not be confused with the creation of a federal state. For that would require the transfer to the Union of predominant responsibility for the armed forces as a whole: a completely different matter from a rapid reaction force of modest dimensions.

If the Union does develop an effective defence capacity, it will become something more than a great civilian power. But the uncertainty of that prospect makes it all the more necessary to build on the proven capacity in the economic and environmental aspects of external policy. The impact of the Union on the outside world, with or without a defence capacity, will be enhanced as it enlarges to include Central and Eastern Europe, leading to a population of some half a billion: but only on condition that its institutions, and particularly those of the central, Community pillar, are strengthened rather than weakened. If enlargement were to weaken the Union's institutions, it would become an inert mass that could stand in the way of global stability and prosperity: something much less than a great civilian power. But enlargement that strengthens the Union would enable it to carry yet greater weight in world affairs than it has done hitherto.

Chapter 9
The EU and the rest of Europe

The name the founding fathers gave the European Community expressed an aspiration, not a fact. Six countries in the middle of Western Europe, however important, could hardly be called Europe. But the aspiration, shared by most federalists, was that the Community would grow until the name became genuinely appropriate. With the enlargement, first to include almost all of Western Europe, and in the coming years most Central and East European countries, the aspiration is approaching reality. Meanwhile there are external relations with those preparing to join that have not yet done so and, in a different perspective, with the rest of Europe.

Most candidates for membership have sought economic advantage and political influence. For Greece, Portugal, and Spain the consolidation of their democracies was also a motive. The same is true of most Central and East European countries that wish to join the European mainstream after the long years under Soviet domination; and they hope too for enhanced security.

Member states generally agree that the Eastern enlargement is to be welcomed, to extend the area of prosperity and security, and as a natural destination for the European Union. For Germany in particular it is essential for stability and security among the Eastern neighbours. Many among the British have hoped, like Mrs Thatcher, that it will result in 'looser', more intergovernmental institutions. The French in particular have on the contrary feared that widening will dilute the great European project. But all now accept the principle of enlargement to Central and Eastern Europe, if with varying degrees of enthusiasm; and the treaty affirms that membership is open to any European state that respects 'the principles of liberty, democracy, respect for human rights and fundamental freedoms, and the rule of law'.

Enlargement to almost all of Western Europe

There is a routine for the process of enlargement. When an application is received, the Council asks the Commission for its 'Opinion', on the basis of which the Council may, unanimously, approve a mandate for negotiations. The Commission negotiates, supervised by the Council; and an eventual treaty of accession has to be adopted by unanimity in the Council and with the assent of the Parliament, followed by ratification in all the member states.

Membership can be preceded by a form of association. The original example was the Treaty of Association between Greece and the Community in 1962, which provided for the removal of trade barriers over a transitional period, various forms of co-operation, and a Council of Association. It also envisaged eventual membership; and after various vicissitudes, Greece did indeed become a member in 1981.

Turkey soon followed with a similar treaty in 1964, save that the Community's doubts about Turkey were reflected in a transition period of twenty-two years and no clear commitment to membership. The doubts persist to this day, based on concern about human rights, democratic stability, a low level of economic development, and high rate of inflation, combined with a size of population, some 70 million and rising fast, which makes such things harder to accommodate. Turkey lodged its application for membership in 1987, but it was not until 1999 that the Union recognized it as a candidate, though without fixing a date to open negotiations.

Portugal and Spain were not in the 1960s eligible for association. Their regimes were incompatible with the Community, for which only democratic countries were suitable partners; and Portugal had already in 1960 become a founder member of the European Free Trade Association (Efta), which Britain had promoted in reaction to the establishment of the EEC and which, being confined to a purely trading relationship, was not so concerned about the political complexion of its members. So when democracy replaced dictatorship in the 1970s, both Iberian countries negotiated entry to the Community without any prior form of association. This was one reason why the negotiations were protracted, with entry achieved only in 1986. Protectionist resistance, from French farmers in particular, was however more significant.

The path to membership was different for the more northerly members of Efta. The British, Danes, Norwegians, Swedes, and Swiss had eschewed the political implications of Community membership; and the Austrians were precluded by their peace treaty. Britain, Denmark, and Ireland joined in 1973 without having been associated in any way. Bilateral free trade agreements were at the same time concluded between the Community and each of the other Efta states, which by then included Iceland; and they were later signed with Finland, which joined in 1986, and Liechtenstein, in 1991.

As soon as the Soviet constraint was removed in 1989, Austria applied for EC membership. Finland, Norway, Sweden, and Switzerland were not far behind. Delors, hoping to delay such enlargement lest it dilute the Community, devised a proposal for a European Economic Area (EEA) to include the Efta countries with the EC in an extended single market. But the governments of those five did not want to be excluded from decision-taking in the Community and they too applied for membership, which Austria, Finland, and Sweden achieved in 1995,

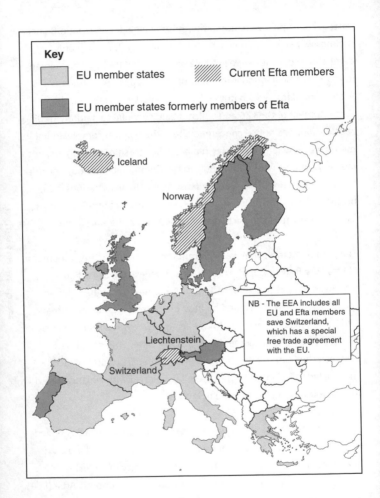

Key

EU member states   Current Efta members

EU member states formerly members of Efta

Iceland

Norway

NB - The EEA includes all EU and Efta members save Switzerland, which has a special free trade agreement with the EU.

Liechtenstein

Switzerland

Map 2. EU, Efta, EEA.

after a short negotiation facilitated by their existing free trade relationship. Norwegians rejected accession in their referendum and Swiss voters refused to accept even the EEA. So Switzerland continues with its bilateral free trade agreement and only a vestigial EEA remains, associating Norway, Iceland, and Liechtenstein with the Union. The Union itself includes all the other countries of Western Europe save Cyprus and Malta, which are negotiating entry.

Enlargement to the East

Throughout the cold war, relations were cool between the EC and the Soviet Union. The Soviet Union refused to accord the Community legal recognition, seeing it as strengthening the 'capitalist camp'; and the Community refused to negotiate with Comecon, the economic organization dominated by the Soviet Union. Following 1989, and the dissolution of the Soviet bloc, the Central and East European countries turned towards the Community, which they saw as a bastion of prosperity and democracy. They naturally envisaged membership.

The simplest case was the German Democratic Republic, as the Soviet-controlled part of Germany had called itself. The GDR became part of the Federal Republic of Germany in 1990; and the Community made the necessary technical adjustments at speed so that the enlarged Germany could assume the German membership without delay.

The Community responded to the other emergent democracies of Central and Eastern Europe with association agreements and aid. Aid came in the PHARE programme, designed to help the process of transformation in Central and Eastern Europe. The focus has been on technical assistance for economic reform and structural adjustment, for example education and training, and restructuring in agriculture and the private sector in general. Spending on infrastructure has grown to become the largest single item; and there has been growing emphasis

16. The Wall comes down: Berlin 1989.

on preparing for the single market. Some €1 billion a year have been allocated for PHARE in the Community budget, together with contributions from the member states and from elsewhere. The Community's European Investment Bank has also been financing projects in the region, as has the European Bank for Reconstruction and Development which was established to promote investment in the former Soviet bloc in the private as well as the public sector. Other financial assistance included writing off some half of the external debt of $44 billion which Poland's communist regime had left behind.

While criticized for being less generous than the Marshall Aid to Western Europe after World War Two, all this was of considerable help. But the association treaties, called Europe Agreements, were crucial. The Community had offered them already in 1990 to countries embarking on transformation to market economies and pluralist

The EU's PHARE expenditure by destination, 1990–1998

(million euros)

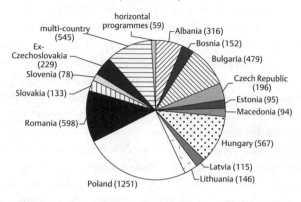

PHARE expenditure by sector, 1990–1998

(million euros)

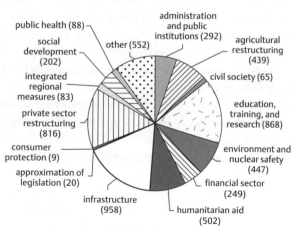

average annual expenditure €621 m

democracies; and by 1996 they had been concluded with all ten of the Central and East European countries that are now negotiating accession. The agreements provided for industrial free trade by stages over transition periods of up to ten years; some reduction of agricultural protection; and liberalization of trade in services, of capital movement, and of the establishment of businesses. Trade has responded well and, bolstered by the prospect of membership, so has foreign investment in the countries with sound economies. There is also provision for 'co-operation' in a wide range of fields, which depends largely on the PHARE assistance. There are institutions to supervise the working of each agreement and provide a forum for political dialogue: a Council of Association with representatives of the Commission and of governments of member states and the associate; a Committee of Association, with high officials from each side; and a Parliamentary Association Committee, with MEPs and MPs from the associate.

While the first candidates for association wanted the agreements to recognize eventual membership as an objective, member states were divided about it, with France especially doubtful. So the agreements were equivocal on the subject. But France too came round and by 1993 the right to negotiate for accession was offered to those that fulfilled certain conditions: stable democracy, human rights and protection of minorities, the rule of law, a competitive market economy, and 'ability to take on the obligations of membership including adherence to the aims of political, economic and monetary union'. While political union meant different things in different member states, the significance of 'the obligations of membership' was clear enough, including the huge task of applying not far short of 100,000 pages of legislation, mostly concerning the single market. To allay fears that widening would result in weakening, there was also the condition that the Union should have 'the capacity to absorb new members while maintaining the momentum of integration'.

Hungary and Poland lodged their applications for accession in the

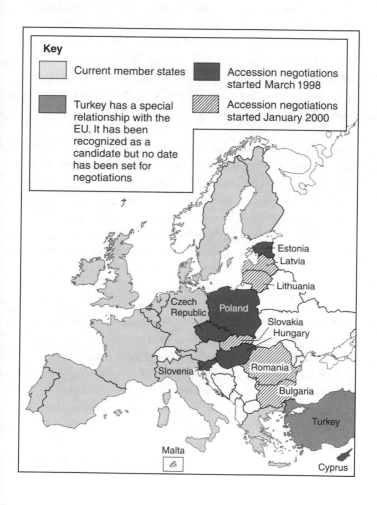

Key

Current member states

Accession negotiations started March 1998

Turkey has a special relationship with the EU. It has been recognized as a candidate but no date has been set for negotiations

Accession negotiations started January 2000

Estonia
Latvia
Lithuania
Czech Republic
Poland
Slovakia
Hungary
Slovenia
Romania
Bulgaria
Turkey
Malta
Cyprus

Map 3. Applicants for accession.

following year and by 1996 eight more of the Central and East European states had done so. By 1998 the Union judged that a first wave of five had made the necessary progress, so negotiations began in 1998 with the Czech Republic, Estonia, Hungary, Poland, and Slovenia, as well as Cyprus which had also applied to join; and, in 2000, also with a second wave comprising Bulgaria, Latvia, Lithuania, Romania, and Slovakia, as well as Malta. Allowing time for completion of the negotiations, then assent and ratification, the first accessions are expected around 2004.

Meanwhile the Union was making some progress with its own 'capacity to absorb new members'. The common agricultural policy required reform to cope with the addition of a large number of farmers from the East; and the financial perspective for 2000–6 had to provide for bigger structural funds. The European Council in Berlin in March 1999, with the newly elected Gerhard Schröder as President-in-Office, took some of the necessary decisions. The budget for structural funds was increased and CAP prices were cut though, as we saw in Chapter 5, not enough. Another round of cuts will be necessary.

Along with the allocation to the structural funds for new member states, rising from €5.8 billion in 2003 to €12.1 billion in 2006, together with agricultural support rising to €3.4 billion, there is €3.1 billion a year of 'pre-accession aid' for the remaining candidates. These sums may be found insufficient. Among the first wave of candidates, Poland and Estonia, though growing fast, average less than half of the Union's GDP per head; and among the second wave, Bulgaria, Latvia, Lithuania, and Romania average only about a quarter. Much remains to be done to ensure that such disparities do not place the Union under too much strain.

The reform of the Union's institutions is yet more essential. For as the number of member states exceeds twenty, rising towards thirty or more, timely and effective decisions will become less and less feasible in those fields where the intergovernmental element predominates and the veto remains. The IGC 2000 was intended to prepare the institutions for enlargement; and it did reach decisions on matters such as limiting the number of Commissioners and reweighting the votes in the Council towards the larger states. But the Nice Treaty did not reduce the scope for unanimous voting enough to ensure effective decision-taking, nor was co-decision of Council and Parliament made the norm in line with standard democratic procedures. Unless this is done, however, at least for the Community pillar, the prospects for the Union, as the number of member states rises from the next enlargement onwards, will not be good.

GDP per head in the EU and applicant states
($ '000s, purchasing power parities, 1997)

Luxembourg	30.2*	Cyprus	14.8
Denmark	23.6	Malta	13.2
Belgium	22.8	Slovenia	11.8
Austria	22.1	Czech Republic	10.5
France	22.0	Slovakia	7.9
Germany	21.3	Hungary	7.5
Netherlands	21.1	Poland	6.5
United Kingdom	20.7	Turkey	6.4
Ireland	20.7	Estonia	5.2
Italy	20.3	Romania	4.3
Finland	20.2	Lithuania	4.2
Sweden	19.8	Bulgaria	4.1
Spain	15.9	Latvia	3.9
Portugal	14.3	* 1996	
Greece	12.5	(source: World Bank)	

The West Balkans

The West Balkans denotes mainly the states of former Yugoslavia: Croatia, Bosnia-Hercegovina, Macedonia, and the present Yugoslavia comprising Montenegro and Serbia, of which Kosovo remains formally a province. Albania is also included within the term, but in current discussions of EU policy Slovenia is not because, though it was also one of the former Yugoslav republics, it has qualified to become an associate and a candidate for membership.

Before it disintegrated, the former Yugoslavia had been closer to the Community than any other Central or East European state. Then came the disintegration and the wars. The United States initially wanted the Europeans to deal with the problems. Jacques Poos, Luxembourg's Foreign Minister and President-in-Office of the Council in the first half of 1991, famously said 'This is the hour of Europe . . .' before setting out to visit Yugoslavia where, in both Croatia and Slovenia, conflicts had already broken out. Not having a significant Serb minority, Slovenia secured independence without much fighting. But bitter wars ensued in Croatia, Bosnia, and Kosovo, where there were large, geographically concentrated Serb minorities. The following years were to demonstrate that the Union, despite its strength in the economic field, was unable to respond effectively to the use of force. Poos had added to his famous sentence: ' . . . it is not the hour of the Americans'. But he was utterly mistaken. Even though the British and French supplied the largest contingents of troops in Bosnia, the decade of the 1990s was to be the time of the United States. It was certainly not the time of the Organization for Security and Co-operation in Europe (at first called Conference – CSCE, rather than OSCE) or of the United Nations; and while the EU's economic and humanitarian contribution was important, in a decade dominated by three wars it was eclipsed by Nato and, above all, the USA.

The European Political Co-operation, useful though it was in less fraught matters, was unable to cope with the issue of recognition of Croatia and Slovenia as independent states. Although the British, French, and most other member state governments thought early recognition dangerous, Germany and one or two others leant towards independence. The German government made it increasingly clear through 1990 that, whatever other member states might wish, it would recognize them both, and so it did in December. The others then decided to follow in order not to show a split within the EPC; and this may have contributed to the outbreak of violence and subsequent wars. One may conclude that political recognition, at least by the Union if not yet by the member states, should become a Union competence, decided by qualified majority vote.

It has also been suggested that the costs arising from the wars and the damage to the Union's reputation might have been avoided by timely intervention to deal with the former Yugoslavia's pressing economic problems, including a massive debt. The EU has since been the biggest supplier of aid, contributing around €1 billion a year. It has also helped with civilian peace-keeping, such as monitoring elections, deploying and training police, clearing mines, counter-terrorism, and assistance for institution-building. Patten has accordingly proposed an EU 'non-military rapid reaction facility', available to help prevent conflicts by building on the existing strengths of the Union, along with the creation of the military rapid reaction force that is to be created by 2003.

More generally, Patten and Solana presented a joint report to the European Council in March 2000, drawing lessons from the EU's experience in the West Balkans. They criticized the decision-taking as slow and cumbersome, with two committees of officials from member states involved before a proposal comes to the Council, where the unanimity procedure leads to action at the level of the 'lowest common denominator'. Efforts had been dispersed because member states' programmes were not integrated with those of the Union. Most damagingly, the Union did not deliver on its promises rapidly and efficiently, because of the budgetary procedures outlined in Chapter 8: governments did not promptly pay their agreed shares; nor was the Council's wish to finance such expenditures out of the routine CFSP budget, which did not allow for them, compatible with rapid reaction to emergencies.

Now, after three wars, the EU has initiated a Stability Pact for South-East Europe, to be followed by Stability and Association Agreements between the Union and each of the West Balkan states, including the present Yugoslavia provided that democracy is firmly established there. This is backed by an aid programme for the West Balkans envisaged at some €5.5 billion for the years 2000–6. Half is to come from the Union's budget and half from the member states; and two-fifths is reserved for a democratic Serbia. The estimated cost to member states of the Kosovo war and peace-keeping in 1999–2000 was not much less than the whole budget for the 2000–6 programme; and the damage to the Union's reputation of further failure in this vital area of the CFSP would be very great, not to speak of the damage to citizens in the West Balkans. The risk of this is compounded by every month of delay. Yet so far the taking of decisions to allocate money has remained agonizingly slow.

Provided that peace prevails, however, the Stability and Association Agreements together with the aid programme should set these states on course for eventual membership of the Union, following the example of the other Central and East Europeans; and this should ensure their continuing peace and prosperity, so long as the Union itself has been strengthened enough to cope with over thirty member states.

Russia and the CIS

The three Baltic republics of the former Soviet Union, Estonia, Latvia, and Lithuania, declined to join Russia in the successor Commonwealth of Independent States (CIS) and are negotiating entry into the European

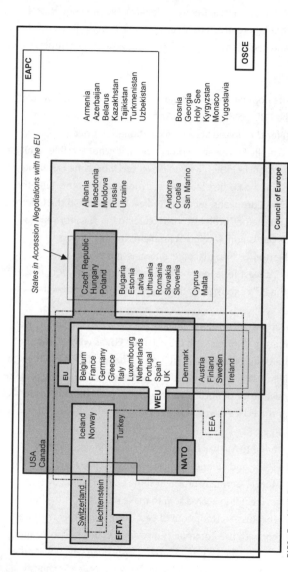

EAPC

Council of Europe

OSCE

States in Accession Negotiations with the EU

Albania
Macedonia
Moldova
Russia
Ukraine

Andorra
Croatia
San Marino

Armenia
Azerbaijan
Belarus
Kazakhstan
Tajikistan
Turkmenistan
Uzbekistan

Bosnia
Georgia
Holy See
Monaco
Kyrgyzstan
Yugoslavia

Czech Republic
Hungary
Poland

Bulgaria
Estonia
Latvia
Lithuania
Romania
Slovakia
Slovenia

Cyprus
Malta

EU

Belgium
France
Germany
Greece
Italy
Luxembourg
Netherlands
Portugal
Spain
UK

Denmark

WEU

Austria
Finland
Sweden

Ireland

EEA

USA
Canada

Iceland
Norway

Turkey

NATO

Switzerland

Liechtenstein

EFTA

EAPC = Euro-Atlantic Partnership Council; EEA = European Economic Area; EFTA = European Free Trade Area; EU = European Union; NATO = North Atlantic Treaty Organisation;
OSCE = Organization for Security and Co-operation in Europe; WEU = Western European Union.

Map 4. The architecture of Europe.

Union. Among the states that stayed with the CIS, six can claim to be European: Armenia, Belarus, Georgia, Moldova, Ukraine, and Russia itself. They could therefore, if they come to fulfil the conditions of stable democracy and competitive market economy, apply for membership of the EU.

Russia, with its population around 150 million, is so big that it would unbalance the EU's political system. So accession is scarcely more feasible than for the United States which, though not geographically in Europe, is culturally European: in other words, it is not feasible. While it is conceivable that the other five could eventually become candidates for membership, the EU first faces an enormous task in absorbing the Central and East Europeans, let alone Turkey. Europeans in the CIS, for their part, with their difficult histories including the seventy years as part of the Soviet Union, face great problems in their efforts to transform themselves into market economies and pluralist democracies. At least for a long time ahead they must be regarded as partners in the EU's external relations, not potential member states.

Ukraine is a large state with a population of some fifty million, which will have common frontiers with the enlarged EU, as will Belarus and Moldova. The Union should do what it can to foster stability in these states. But it is Russia, with its great problems and great potential, along with its massive stock of nuclear weapons, that presents the major challenge for the EU's external relations.

The EU responded to Mikhail Gorbachev's liberalizing reforms by concluding a trade and co-operation agreement in 1990 and granting financial assistance. Germany provided some ecu 40 billion over the next five years, including a large sum to make it worth Gorbachev's while to pull the Russian troops out of East Germany. Other member states, together with the Community, provided ecu 15 billion. In 1991 the Community launched a programme of assistance which was, after the disintegration of the Soviet Union in that year, called Technical

Assistance to the Commonwealth of Independent States (TACIS). With a budget of around half a billion ecus a year, one-third of it for Russia, a tenth for Ukraine, over a quarter for regional programmes, and the rest for the eleven other CIS states, TACIS concentrated on such things as enterprise restructuring and development, administrative reform, social services, education, and, as the biggest item, nuclear safety, which accounts for a large part of the regional programmes.

Access to the Union's market has presented few problems to Russia, as Russian exports have largely been oil, gas, timber, diamonds, and other materials on which the EU does not impose tariffs or quotas, though anti-dumping duties have been charged on products such as steel. But in order to encourage exports of manufactures, the EU offered the CIS states tariff preferences. Wide-ranging Partnership and Co-operation Agreements somewhat similar to the Europe Agreements were then concluded between the EU and CIS states. But there are crucial

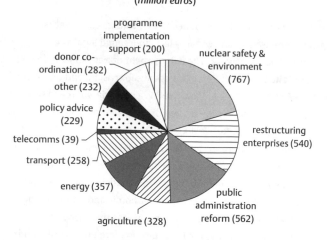

TACIS spending by sector, 1991–1997
(*million euros*)

programme implementation support (200)

donor co-ordination (282)

other (232)

policy advice (229)

telecomms (39)

transport (258)

energy (357)

agriculture (328)

nuclear safety & environment (767)

restructuring enterprises (540)

public administration reform (562)

average annual expenditure €542 m

CIS states with EU agreements

The EU has Partnership and Co-operation Agreements with:

Armenia	Kazakhstan	Russian Federation
Azerbaijan	Kyrgyzstan	Ukraine
Belarus	Moldova	Uzbekistan
Georgia		

differences: free trade was offered only 'eventually', when the economic transformation is further advanced; as the co-operation mentioned in the agreements depends largely on TACIS, which is on a smaller scale than PHARE, it is accordingly more modest; there is no mention of membership; and without the prospect of membership, the institutions of association, though similar to those of the Europe Agreements, have less substance to discuss – though given the importance of EU–Russian relations, the association with Russia should be an exception.

Relations with Russia have not been easy, with its combination of unstable politics and an economy lacking a sound legal and administrative framework. The enlargement of Nato to include Poland, Hungary, and the Czech Republic has caused tension; and the possibility that the Baltic states may follow them is a potential source of strain. The EU for its part has found the degree of violence employed by Russia in Chechnya distasteful. Russia does not, however, view the EU and its enlargement unfavourably; and the EU would benefit greatly from good relations with a stable and viable Russia. Much depends on how far and how fast Russia, with Vladimir Putin a more efficient president than Boris Yeltsin, can make the necessary economic and political progress. But to make a significant contribution towards this is one of the principal challenges facing the EU's common foreign, security, and above all external economic policy.

If a genuine partnership can be forged with Russia, it would be a most important element in the EU's European policy and its relationship with the wider world.

Chapter 10
The EU and the world

Having shown how 'federal institutions can unite highly developed states', the Community might serve as an example of how 'to create a more prosperous and peaceful world'. Such was the hope that Jean Monnet expressed in 1954 to the students of Columbia University in New York. Few now conceive of such an exalted aim. The EU has been concerned, like others, to look after its own interests. But these do include the creation of a prosperous and peaceful world. How far have its actions, as distinct from its example, contributed to that end?

The Community as a trading power

The United States sponsored the uniting of Europe, from Marshall Aid to the birth and early development of the Community. Monnet reciprocated with the idea of an increasingly equal EC–US partnership. Soon after the EEC was founded with its common external tariff, the USA responded by initiating the Kennedy Round of trade liberalization in the Gatt; and this led in 1967, after five years of laborious negotiations, to the agreement to cut tariffs by one-third.

That would have been out of the question had the Community not become, with its common tariff as an instrument of external policy, a trading partner on level terms with the USA. As an observer in Washington put it, the EC was 'now the most important member of

Gatt', and the key to further efforts to liberalize trade. So it indeed became in later rounds of Gatt negotiations, as the creative American impulse of the post-war period declined. The Community played its leading part in the most recent round, opened in Uruguay in 1986 and concluded in 1994. With tariffs on most manufactures already low, the focus moved to non-tariff barriers where the single market programme gave the Community a unique experience in techniques of liberalization. Its experience was also relevant to the replacement of the Gatt by the World Trade Organization, with its wider scope, including trade in services, and greater powers for resolving disputes: a step, perhaps, towards validating the suggestion that the EC's 'example of effective international law-making' might at some stage be 'replicated at global level'.

Of course the Community's trade relations were not all sweetness and light. Far from it. There has been the normal clash of interests, or at least of what participants suppose to be their interests, with agriculture the prime bone of contention. The protectionist common agricultural policy damaged trading partners such as Australia, Canada, New Zealand, and the USA. This was particularly harmful to the first three which, under the system of Commonwealth preference, had enjoyed free entry for their exports to Britain and which, with a few exceptions such as a quota for New Zealand butter, faced the full rigour of the protectionist common agricultural policy after Britain joined the Community: a blow that could have been avoided had Britain not failed to join when the Rome Treaty was negotiated. The damage continued unabated until the Community began to carry out serious reform during the 1990s when it cut the level of protection for some major items by about half. It was agreed in the Uruguay Round that the trade-disrupting export subsidies would be eliminated in the following round: a tough challenge for the Community.

While moving closer together on agriculture, the Community and the USA have been diverging over environmental, cultural, and consumer protection issues, with the Europeans favouring standards which lead to restriction of their imports from the USA and which the Americans regard as protectionist. Genetically modified organisms, hormone-treated beef, noisy aero-engines, data privacy, and films and television programmes are cases in point. It is to be hoped that the WTO will develop a regulatory framework that will help to keep such conflicts within bounds.

The friction induced by the Community's network of preferential arrangements has, on the contrary, been eased as tariffs were reduced in successive Gatt rounds. That network had become so extensive, covering almost the whole of Europe and the Third World, that only a few countries remained outside it, including Australia, Canada, Japan, New Zealand, South Africa, and the USA. The Americans were irked by the EC's preferences for particular countries. But the other side of this coin was the relationships that the EC established with large parts of the Third World. One test of their value could be the contribution that the Union may make to relaunching the first round of negotiations in the framework of the WTO, following the first meeting in Seattle towards the end of 1999 which broke up without agreement largely because of differences between those, including the USA and the EU, that wanted to include environmental and labour standards on the agenda, and Third World countries that did not.

EC, Lomé Convention, Euro-Mediterranean process

Whereas relations with the USA are important for all member states, individual states have special relationships with particular countries in most of the rest of the world; and many of these became shared by the Community as a whole.

This, like much else, stems from the Treaty of Rome. France wanted advantages for its colonies, and made this a condition for ratification of the treaty. So the Community as a whole granted free entry to imports

Directions of EU trade in goods by region, 1998

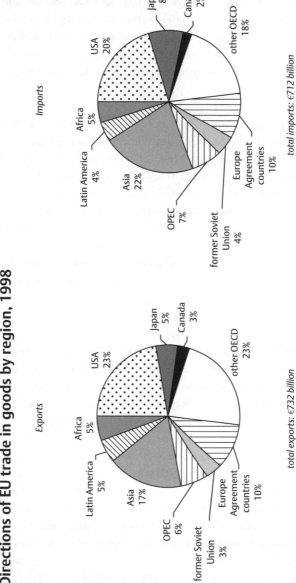

Exports

USA 23%
Japan 5%
Canada 3%
other OECD 23%
Africa 5%
Latin America 5%
Asia 17%
OPEC 6%
former Soviet Union 3%
Europe Agreement countries 10%

total exports: €732 billion

Imports

Japan 8%
Canada 2%
other OECD 18%
USA 20%
Africa 5%
Latin America 4%
Asia 22%
OPEC 7%
former Soviet Union 4%
Europe Agreement countries 10%

total imports: €712 billion

from them and provided aid through the European Development Fund (EDF). The same applied to territories relating to Belgium, Italy, and the Netherlands; and the resulting association was the original basis for the present Lomé Convention. French pressure also led to preferential agreements for Morocco and Tunisia; and these were the forerunners of the present far-reaching system of agreements with Mediterranean states.

After they became independent, the association with former colonies was transmuted through a Convention that provided for joint institutions: a Council of Ministers, Committee of Ambassadors, and Assembly of Parliamentarians. Following British accession, the Commonwealth countries of Africa, the Caribbean, and the Pacific joined in negotiating the Lomé Convention. This broadened the participation to include most of Africa and the Caribbean islands, as well as a number of islands in the Pacific, known collectively as the ACP countries. It removed some vestiges of the colonial system and expanded the aid towards a level of €3 billion a year by the 1990s, together with money to cushion the associates against falls in their income from commodity exports.

Participation in the Lomé Convention was popular and the number of associates grew to seventy-one by the turn of the century, with the whole of Africa already associated, save South Africa and the Mediterranean countries. When South Africa, with its relatively advanced economy, qualified for a formal relationship after abandoning apartheid, a bilateral trade and co-operation agreement was considered more appropriate than the Lomé Convention. Such an agreement can contribute to success for the South African economy, which is crucial for the future of southern Africa and for race relations in the wider world. But the negotiations for the agreement dragged on for five years because the EU's institutions for foreign policy were too weak to convert even such a clear political priority into the necessary action.

The EU's partners in the Lomé Convention

The Lomé Convention links the EU to 71 African, Caribbean, and Pacific (ACP) states, giving them free and preferential entry for their exports to the EU and aid for their economic and social development:

Angola
Antigua and
  Barbuda
Bahamas
Barbados
Belize
Benin
Botswana
Burkina Faso
Burundi
Cabo Verde
Cameroun
Central African
  Republic
Chad
Comores
Congo
Congo Democratic
  Republic
Côte D'Ivoire
Cuba
Djibouti
Dominica
Dominican Republic
Equatorial Guinea
Eritrea

Ethiopia
Fiji
Gabon
Gambia, The
Ghana
Grenada
Guinea
Guinea-Bissau
Guyana
Haiti
Jamaica
Kenya
Kiribati
Lesotho
Liberia
Madagascar
Malawi
Mali
Mauritania
Mauritius
Mozambique
Namibia
Niger
Nigeria
Papua New Guinea
Rwanda

São Tomé & Príncipe
Sénégal
Seychelles
Sierra Leone
Solomon Islands
Somalia
St Kitts and Nevis
St Lucia
St Vincent and The
  Grenadines
Sudan
Suriname
Swaziland
Tanzania
Togo
Tonga
Trinidad and Tobago
Tuvalu
Uganda
Vanuatu
Western Samoa
Zambia
Zimbabwe

The Lomé Convention was renewed for the fifth time in the year 2000, in difficult circumstances. For the associates were disturbed by the erosion of the margins of preference as tariffs had been reduced in successive Gatt rounds; and the Union was concerned that, despite the massive quantities of aid, almost all of Africa remained in bad shape, owing at least partly to poor governance. Enough was at stake, however, to win the agreement to the fifth Convention, both of the EU's partners, with the renewal of the aid programme, and of its member states, with the Convention's recognition that adequate performance in governance would be a criterion for the allocation of aid, and that the associates were to prepare their economies to join the Union in a free trade area in twenty years' time. Through the 1990s, moreover, the EU laid growing emphasis in its external relations on human rights, and the Lomé Convention requires the participants to respect them.

By the end of the 1970s the Community also had a network of agreements according preferences and assistance to states around the Mediterranean, with content not unlike that of the Lomé Convention but without the multilateral institutions. The network included all the North African states – save Libya which declined to participate – together with Israel, Lebanon, and, at one remove from the Mediterranean, Jordan and Syria.

By the 1990s, a combination of economic difficulties, political instability, and rapid population growth in most of these countries, with consequent pressure to migrate to Europe, caused growing anxiety in the Union, particularly among its Southern states. The chance for vigorous action came following the Union's decision to offer accession to Central and East Europeans. This seemed of less vital concern to France, Spain, and Portugal than to Germany. So the Germans, in order to bolster their Southern partners' co-operation in the accession policy, were prepared to endorse a big programme of support for the Union's neighbours to the South. The outcome was a conference of ministers

Lomé Convention V, 2000–2020

The EU and ACP (see box, p. 147) states agreed in 2000 to renew the Lomé Convention for the fifth time, for a 20-year period. The Agreement can be revised every five years and the aid protocols are also to be limited to 5-year periods. The ACP–EU Council of Ministers meets yearly to review progress.

- **Trade** is at the heart of the agreement. Negotiations between the EU and each ACP state for 'economic partnership agreements' are to result by 2008 in a new trading arrangement intended to lead to an EU–ACP free trade area by 2020. Meanwhile the free or preferential entry to the EU is to be retained.
- **Aid** has been set at €13.5 billion for the first seven years, on top of €9.5 billion already allocated but not yet spent. Good performance in use of aid is to be rewarded.
- **Poverty reduction** is to be a favoured focus for development strategies.
- **Non-state actors** are to be encouraged to participate in the development process.
- **Political dialogue** indicates a harder-nosed EU approach, with good governance, respect for human rights, democratic principles, and the rule of law as criteria for aid policy, and with action against corruption.

Lomé V is coloured by the EU's disappointment with the results of the preceding Lomé I–IV, attributed to poor governance in many countries. Given this starting point, the development of an EU–ACP free trade area is a very ambitious idea.

The EU's partners in Euro-Med

The European-Mediterranean Conference includes the EU and 12 Mediterranean states, with the aim of creating a free trade area by 2005:

Algeria	Jordan	Palestinian Authority
Cyprus	Lebanon	Syria
Egypt	Malta	Tunisia
Israel	Morocco	Turkey

Libya has observer status.

from the Union and its Mediterranean partners, held in Barcelona in 1995, which launched a 'Euro-Mediterranean process'.

Among the Union's contributions to the process were a consolidation of the preferences accorded to its Mediterranean partners and an aid programme of some €1 billion a year, while the partners agreed to prepare themselves over a ten-year period to join in a Euro-Mediterranean free trade area. The process also envisaged joint meetings of ministers, but these proved difficult to assemble, given the political divergences among the partner states. The Union itself has concentrated much diplomatic effort on relations with the region, which it must be hoped will prove productive, while not deflecting too much attention from the rest of the Third World.

Asia, Latin America, and generalized preferences

Britain, on joining the Community, managed to secure satisfactory terms for Commonwealth countries from Africa, the Caribbean, and the Pacific. But no special arrangement was agreed for the Asian members of the Commonwealth – India, Pakistan (which then included Bangladesh), Sri Lanka, Malaysia, Hong Kong, and Singapore – most of whose exports had entered Britain tariff-free under Commonwealth preference. The damage was limited, however, because in 1971 the Community was among the first to adopt a Generalized System of Preferences (GSP), according preferential entry to imports from almost all Third World countries that did not already benefit from the Lomé Convention or the Mediterranean agreements; and this reduced the discrimination against most Asian and Latin American countries. The system was less favourable than it may sound because for 'sensitive' (that is, the more competitive) products there were quotas limiting the preferences to quantities fixed in advance for each product and each member state. But the generalized preferences nevertheless helped to strengthen links with Third World countries.

While the margins of preference that the GSP affords Third World countries have declined along with the reduction of the general level of tariffs, their links with the EU through its aid programmes have become increasingly important. By the late 1990s these amounted to some

Shares of official development aid from EU, USA, Japan, and others, 1997

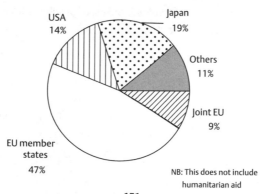

USA
14%

Japan
19%

Others
11%

Joint EU
9%

EU member
states
47%

NB: This does not include
humanitarian aid

Development aid from EU and member states by destination, 1997

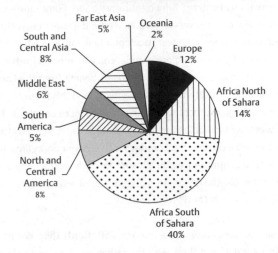

Far East Asia 5%
Oceania 2%
South and Central Asia 8%
Europe 12%
Middle East 6%
Africa North of Sahara 14%
South America 5%
North and Central America 8%
Africa South of Sahara 40%

€6 billion a year, including both humanitarian aid and the development aid for ACP countries and Euro-Med. The Community has also concluded bilateral trade and co-operation agreements to strengthen its links with major Third World countries, including India, Mexico, and Brazil; it has agreements with regional groups such as ASEAN (the Association of South-East Asian Nations); and since Portugal and Spain joined the Community in 1986, their special links with Latin America have been added to those of other member states in Africa and Asia.

While the economic impact of the agreements, preferences, and aid can hardly be measured and may not have been very great, the Union has gained political credit which may be of help in the future development of its relationships with countries of the Third World.

EU agreements and links in the Third World, other than Lomé and Euro-Med

The EU has Trade and Co-operation Agreements with:

Argentina	Mexico	South Korea
Brazil	Pakistan	Sri Lanka
Chile	Paraguay	Uruguay
Colombia	South Africa	Vietnam
India		

The EU has links with other regional groupings, including:

Andean Community (South America)	Gulf Co-operation Council
Mercosur (South America)	ASEAN (Association of South East Asian Nations)
San José group (Central America)	SAARC (South Asian Association for Regional Co-operation)

The EU's Generalized System of Preferences applies to almost all Third World countries.

Money, security, environment

Whereas its common tariff had made the Community a trading power equivalent to the USA, before the euro it had no monetary instrument that could become the equal of the dollar in the international monetary system. The challenge to American hegemony was one of the motives behind the long-standing French support for a single currency. The fluctuations of dollar exchange rates were uncomfortable for other member states too. The dollar's weakness first disrupted the attempt to create a single currency in the early 1970s, then spurred Europeans into taking the first major step of monetary integration with the establishment of the European Monetary System in 1979. In the 1980s the US policy of high interest rates, designed to counter inflation, provoked a debt crisis in many Third World countries, restricting their development for up to a decade.

When those who manage a dominant currency have to choose between dealing with a domestic problem and taking account of the impact on other economies that are influenced by their choice, they naturally choose their domestic interests. Europeans experienced this in the 1990s when high German interest rates, designed to control inflation following German unification, exacerbated recession in other countries influenced by the dominant deutschmark; and this gave added edge to their support for the single currency, with a monetary policy tailored to the needs of the participants as a whole. While that remedy is not available to deal with the dollar's dominance in the world system, the countervailing influence of the euro can offer a second-best solution.

Thus the euro is another source of money with a different economic cycle, which can counteract the dollar's influence when it works against other countries' interests. More positively, the euro could, although the Union's monetary policies have initially been inward-looking, become the basis for an exchange-rate policy that favours international monetary stability. But it is handicapped by the weakness of its arrangements for conducting such a policy, with responsibility divided between the European Central Bank and the Council of finance ministers. The euro might, moreover, along with the dollar and the yen, help to initiate an international system for stabilizing exchange rates. But here its institutional weakness is compounded by the veto that each minister retains over such decisions. The Union will be unable to act responsibly in the international monetary system without appropriate institutional reform. Nor is it likely to exert its due influence in the International Monetary Fund, where the member states taken together have not far short of twice the voting power of the USA, until they come to present a common policy there with a single voice. So it may be some time before the Union can make full use of the opportunity that the euro offers to replace American hegemony with a more equal relationship, such as the common commercial policy has long since done with respect to trade.

American hegemony in defence will, however, remain unchallenged for as long ahead as can be contemplated. Not only would Europeans have to undertake vast expenditure in any attempt to become independent of American strategic power, but the force thus acquired would also have to be controlled by a solidly established democratic European state with a number of years of reliable decision-taking behind it. So Europeans continue to need Nato's American-led strategic shield; and their efforts in the field of defence will be confined to a capacity to contribute to peace-keeping and, more ambitiously, peace-making, particularly in actions sponsored by the United Nations. For defence of the Union's territory against any serious threats, Europeans will continue to depend on American protection.

Soft security, other than that requiring military force, is quite another matter. The Union is well placed to contribute to conflict prevention and peace-keeping with civilian means. It has gained relevant experience in the former Yugoslavia, on the basis of which facilities such as the non-military rapid reaction capacity proposed by Patten can readily be constructed. Common positions of the type reached through the CFSP can also be of use. But the Union's capacity to use common instruments such as a civilian rapid reaction facility will remain seriously flawed unless it makes better arrangements for financing them and the veto is removed from decisions on their use.

The environment can also be seen as a vital aspect of security, since global warming and destruction of the ozone layer are among the gravest threats to the welfare, and perhaps the lives, of the world's people. As we saw in Chapter 6, the Union has made the major contribution to international efforts to deal with these problems, taking the initiative for the control of CFCs that destroy the ozone layer and performing the leading role in the negotiations at Kyoto to limit the use of the 'greenhouse gases' that cause global warming, particularly carbon dioxide (CO_2) released by the use of coal and oil. The Americans' reluctance was a principal reason why the agreement reached at Kyoto provided for only about half the cuts that the EU had proposed. The USA also made ratification of the agreement conditional on its acceptance by Third World countries. But the largest of these resisted acceptance unless enough aid was provided to help them adopt the necessary eco-friendly technologies with which to continue their economic development; and the Americans declined to accept that condition. The EU, with its close relations with many Third World countries, may be better placed to appreciate the need to combine control of CO_2 emissions with assistance for sustainable development.

The Union itself is not certain to implement its cuts, since the decisions it has taken are not legally enforceable in the member states; and its arrangements for negotiating internationally are weakened by the veto that applies to important decisions about CO_2. Yet the negotiations at Kyoto demonstrated its potential in this field. With Germans and Scandinavians in the lead, Europeans are among those most conscious of environmental issues; and given appropriate institutional reform, the Union could apply its full weight to secure international agreement for dealing with what may otherwise become an insoluble problem.

The Union's role in the world

Too much American hegemony is dangerous for the Americans as well as for others. The burden is too great for one country to carry alone. Only the EU has the potential to be at least an equal partner with respect to the economy, the environment, and soft security, though not defence. The EU's achievement in the world trading system has shown what can be done when effective institutions dispose of a common instrument.

17. Two Presidents meet: Clinton and Delors.

The euro offers a basis for a similar performance in the international monetary system, but only if the institutions for external monetary policy are adequately reformed. For action on the global environment the Union is fairly well equipped, though here again its powers need to be strengthened. Soft security, including the civilian aspects of keeping the peace, is a field in which the Union is developing a capacity that could become an essential counterpart to the unrivalled American military power; and the military instruments that the EU is creating also open up the opportunity to perform a complementary role.

Other great powers will emerge in the twenty-first century into what will become a multipolar world. Adjustment to such changes in power relationships is always hard for those who have been on top. It will be easier for the Americans if they have already adjusted to an equal partnership with the EU in other fields as well as trade; and the EU, with its network of relations with countries throughout the South as well as the North of the world, will be well placed to advance the process of creating a stable world system that accommodates the emergent powers.

The Union's own experience of institutions, policies, and attitudes that have helped the member states to live together in peace for half a century, together with its worldwide network of relationships, should enable it to influence others to move in a similar direction. But Monnet's idea that such institutions might serve to create a prosperous and peaceful world could be realized only under quite exacting conditions. The necessary sharing of sovereignty is possible only for pluralist democracies that are willing to accept a common rule of law, and have the capacity to develop common legislative institutions to enact it and a system of government to implement policies within it. These conditions apply to a large extent within the Union, but in many parts of the world they do not. While the Union can help to make the United Nations and other international organizations more effective, global institutions of a community type cannot be created until pluralist democracy becomes the norm throughout the world. But Union policies which point towards such an outcome are in the long-term interest of its states and citizens; and even if a very long time-scale has to be envisaged, the European experience has shown that initiating a process which leads in that direction can already begin to transform relations between states.

Chapter 11
So far so good . . . but what next?

The European Union has come a long way in the half-century since the process of its construction was launched by the Schuman declaration. War has indeed become unthinkable among the member states, which now cover almost the whole of Western Europe and before long will include most of Central and Eastern Europe too. The preceding chapters have shown how, in the course of those fifty years, institutions, powers, and policies have been put in place to deal with matters beyond the reach of governments of the individual states. Now we can try to sum up what has been done and ask what the future may hold.

Do the powers and instruments match the aims?

The Union has been able to achieve its aims where it has powers and instruments with which to act. These can be legislative, such as the framework for the single market; fiscal, as with the budget or the common external tariff; and financial, as the aid programmes and now the single currency. Co-operation based on the powers and instruments of member states can be useful, but would not achieve much without the hard core of common powers and instruments.

The single market legislation provides a framework for economic strength and prosperity, even if it remains incomplete in a few sectors and will need further development to cater for the new economy of e-commerce and information technology; and the single currency completes the single market in the monetary domain, though without, so far, the participation of all member states.

The budget has transferred resources to sectors deemed to require support, originally to agriculture but increasingly to less developed regions and member states. While the agricultural budget has generated conflict, the structural funds to assist development of poorer regions have been more generally favoured. The forthcoming enlargement to Central and Eastern Europe may bring pressure for larger structural funds. But no major increase in the Union's power to obtain tax revenue is likely to be necessary.

Thus the Union does not need much more by way of powers in the economic field. The same can be said of the environment, where the need is to use existing powers to forge a strategy for sustainable development rather than to add new ones.

Social policy as embodied in the welfare state belongs, following the principle of subsidiarity, to the member states. That principle justifies EU involvement in some employment-related aspects of social policy, such as the prevention of social dumping by undercutting standards of health and safety at work. There is a grey area, including elements of social security, where there is conflict between those who want to establish Union-wide standards and those who consider that differences rooted in differing social cultures should not be disturbed. Disagreements remain; but the latter view has been gaining ground.

While the economic and environmental aims and powers were promoted by interest groups as well as federalists, as was the free movement of workers across the internal frontiers, it was the federal idea that lay behind free movement for all within the Union, which has been accepted by member states save Denmark, Ireland, and the UK. But all the states participate in measures to combat cross-frontier crime.

In the field of its external relations, the Union's powers have been designed to defend and promote common interests, which include stability in the international economic and political system. The most potent instrument is the offer of accession, hence of participation in the Union's institutions and powers as a whole, to other European states. This should in a few years' time have enlarged its area of stability and prosperity to encompass most of Europe.

The powers over external trade, together with the instrument of the common external tariff, have enabled the Union to promote its interest in liberal international trade as well as to turn what was American hegemony in this field into EU–US partnership. The protectionist common agricultural policy, working in the opposite direction, marred relations with some trading partners; but though reforms to correct this distortion have taken far too long, they are being accomplished by stages. A combination of preferential arrangements and aid has strengthened links with most Third World countries. Along with this influence in the world trading system, the Union has used its environmental powers to play a leading part in international negotiations to protect the ozone layer and curb global warming.

With the euro the Union has a potentially powerful instrument to wield in the international monetary system. But until it has adequate institutional arrangements for external monetary policy, its potential, which could convert American hegemony into partnership in this field too, is not likely to be realized.

For defence, American military dominance remains a fact which the EU's incremental approach to military integration is not designed to challenge, though it should serve the Union's interests in particular cases. It is in the civil domain that the Union can complement American power, with civilian aspects of peace-keeping and, much more substantially, through its contribution to European and world stability in the economic, environmental, and political fields. The Union is uniquely placed to ease the transition from global American hegemony, via what should become an equal Euro-American partnership in all fields save defence, to the multipolar world system that will have to be developed in the coming years. The Union does not need much by way of new powers to accomplish this. It needs further reform of the institutions to enable it to use the powers it has to good effect.

The institutions: how effective? how democratic?

Eurosceptics tend to regard 'closer integration' as undesirable without distinguishing between transfer of powers to the Union and reform of its institutions. But these are two very different questions. The transfer of powers is justified only where the Union can serve the citizens in ways that individual member states cannot; and the Union already has most of the powers indicated by the subsidiarity principle except in the field of defence. Once powers have been transferred, however, they will not serve the citizens' interests unless they are wielded by effective and democratic Union institutions.

The political institutions require a context of the rule of law, which is ensured by the Court of Justice in matters of Community competence.

The Council, however, is not effective enough where the unanimity rule prevails, as was demonstrated by the inadequacy of single market legislation before qualified majority voting was applied. It has become more effective now that QMV applies to four-fifths of legislation as well as the whole of the budget; but the Nice Treaty goes only part of the way towards the further extension that is needed. Unanimity and enhanced co-operation remain the practical procedures where the Union depends on the use of member states' instruments, as in the field of defence. But as the number of member states grows there must be increasing doubts about the Union's capacity to act where unanimity still applies in matters such as treaties of association and accession, nominations to some major posts in the institutions, and international agreements on exchange rate arrangements.

The Commission has substantial powers to fulfil its functions as the Community's executive, though its role in ensuring that member states do in fact carry out the administration that is delegated to them by the Community is not strong enough, and intervention by the Council and its network of committees in the execution of Community decisions hampers the Commission's effectiveness. The Commission's own administrative culture had also become a serious weakness before the European Parliament secured the Commissioners' resignation in March 1999; but the reforms set in train by the new Commission should bring substantial improvement.

The part the Parliament played in the old Commission's resignation showed how democratic control can contribute to effectiveness. But the Parliament's impact on legislation and on the budget remains limited by the treaty, which puts it on a par with the Council for only some half of each. The Council has retained dominant power over the agricultural half of the budget, where its record can hardly be called distinguished; and the Parliament has performed creditably on the other half of the budget and the half of the legislation that it co-decides on level terms with the Council.

The Nice Treaty does little to increase the scope for co-decision; and this is a very serious omission. For in so far as it remains incomplete the Union will be neglecting an essential means of securing citizens' support. Citizens are likely to become a centrifugal force unless they develop a commitment to the Union alongside that to their states; and it would be unwise to ignore the track record of representative democracy as a major element in citizenship. So long as citizens do not see the Parliament as an equal of the Council, they are not likely to regard it as a sufficiently important channel of representation. The Council, representing the states, is an essential part of the Union's legislature too. But even if it can be brought to hold its legislative sessions in public, it will remain at the centre of an opaque system of quasi-diplomatic negotiation. Representation in a powerful house of the citizens is a condition of their support for the Union over the longer term.

The success of the provision for gender equality at work shows how citizens' rights can also generate support for the Union. The treaty provides for a number of other rights, mostly connected with work, as well as requiring the institutions to respect the European Convention of Human Rights. The Charter of Fundamental Rights that was drafted by a convention of MEPs, MPs, and government representatives and welcomed by the European Council at Nice will be of help to citizens, though the question of the Charter's legal status was left to be decided later. But most important of all for the citizens will be the Union's effectiveness in doing things that are necessary for them. It must be seen to be doing such things at a time when it confronts major challenges, including the impending enlargement.

Flexible versus federal

Flexibility is built into the second pillar, with its common foreign and security policy. Member states can opt into or out of common positions or actions at will. In so far as the CFSP depends on co-operation using the member states' policy instruments, this may be inevitable. But it makes the second pillar much less effective than the Community. The Amsterdam Treaty none the less introduced the procedure called 'enhanced co-operation' to provide for opting into or out of the Community's activities.

Recalling the original launching of the Community, many in the six founder states saw enhanced co-operation as a way ahead again for a core, leaving reluctant partners to catch up later. In this view, the British and the Danes were the main problem, though there have also been fears that Central and East Europeans may impede the Union's development unless a vanguard can proceed without them. But enhanced co-operation as foreseen at Amsterdam and Nice is not likely to lead to a vanguard but rather to opting in or out by differing groups of states. A growing body of legislation applying to various groups of states risks weakening the rule of law within the Community, business efficiency in the single market, and comprehensibility of the Union to its citizens. If the Community already has the essential powers in its fields of competence, it is hard to justify such risks for the sake of lesser initiatives; and the Community does indeed have these powers, with one major exception: the opt-outs from the single currency.

The British opt-out is the key. The effect on Britain of exclusion from the euro is the subject of intense debate, in which this writer's position is clear: Britain should be in. But it must also be realized that abstention of a major member state from its main project weakens the Union too and increases the risk that new member states will follow suit, with a generally disintegrative effect – unless the euro-zone core does in fact constitute an integrative vanguard. Neither a disintegrating Union, and consequently an unstable Europe, nor a Union in which Britain is progressively sidelined, and hence doubtless on bad terms with its partners, would serve a British interest; a free trading relationship with the Union, like that of Norway or Switzerland, would be better.

While opinion polls have shown the British two-to-one against joining the euro, they have also shown that eight out of ten expect it will have happened by 2010. Such passive acceptance rather than active participation has been a normal British reaction to the Union; and citizens' attitudes have reflected politicians' delays in joining the Community and participating in some of the subsequent developments, with damage to the interests of Britain, some Commonwealth countries, and also the Union itself. British participation in the single market project has, on the contrary, been active, with consequent benefits for Britain and other member states; but difficulties due to self-exclusion from the euro may well come to be seen as another case of damage caused by delay.

Since 1997, Tony Blair's government has shown signs of readiness to break the mould of reluctant acceptance and opting out, with the launching of the Anglo-French defence initiative, promoting Union policies to deal with the new economy, and being generally more positive about the Union. It still seems not to be understood, however, that 'closer integration', once the euro is accepted, applies only marginally to the Union's powers, apart from the incremental approach to a role in defence, but mainly to completing the process of making the Community institutions effective and democratic, in which full co-decision for the European Parliament is the most important remaining requirement.

British understanding of the process of reforming the institutions has been clouded by misunderstanding of the word federal, which is generally employed in other member states in its proper sense of democratic government at two or more levels, with the levels of government closer to the citizens, following the principle of subsidiarity, responsible for the functions they can effectively perform.

In Britain, with our particular history of constitutional development, the word constitution can also sound alarming. It is, however, the means of making the principles and rules of the game comprehensible not only to politicians and lawyers but also to other citizens. The essential is to make the Union's institutions effective and democratic. The constitutional elements can then be concentrated in a separate part of the Treaty: surely no cause for alarm. The IGC to be convened in 2004 should help to clarify these institutional questions as well as that of the division of powers between the Union and the states.

Without reform to make the institutions fully effective and democratic, the Union might survive for a long time, if with a declining capacity to serve the interests of its citizens. But it risks stagnation and progressive disintegration. With adequate reforms, the Union has the capacity to provide the framework for Europe's new economy and democratic stability, and to assist the development of a multipolar world system that can deliver security and sustainable development. British people who choose active participation rather than passive acceptance could do a great deal to ensure that this is what does in fact happen.

References

References, in line with the nature of this series, have been kept to the minimum of quotations whose source is not obvious from the text.

Chapter 2
Spinelli called the Single Act a 'dead mouse' in his speech to the European Parliament on 16 January 1986, reprinted in Altiero Spinelli, *Discorsi al Parlamento Europeo*, ed. Pier Virgilio Dastoli (Bologna, 1987), 369. Jenkins recalled his choice of a theme to 'move Europe forward' in *European Diary 1977–1981* (London, 1989), 22–3.

Chapter 3
Margaret Thatcher spoke of 'a European super-state' in her *Britain and Europe: Text of the Speech Delivered in Bruges by the Prime Minister on 20th September 1988* (London: Conservative Political Centre, 1988), 4.

Chapter 7
Bevin and Victoria Station is to be found in Michael Charlton, *The Price of Victory* (London, 1983), 43, 44.

Chapter 9
Poos on 'the hour of Europe' was reported in the *New York Times* (29 June 1991), 4.

Chapter 10

The Community 'as an example' is from Jean Monnet, *Les États-Unis d'Europe ont commencé: Discours et allocutions 1952–1954* (Paris, 1955), 128.

The EC as 'the most important member of Gatt' is from Lawrence B. Krause, *European Economic Integration and the United States* (Washington, DC, 1968), 225.

The EC and 'effective international law-making' is from Tommaso Padoa-Schioppa, *Financial and Monetary Integration in Europe: 1990, 1992 and Beyond* (London and New York, 1990), 28.

Further reading

There is a great deal of academic literature on the European Union, but not so many reliable books for the general reader or for those who are just setting out to acquire academic knowledge.

I hope I may be forgiven for suggesting that among **general introductions** to the subject, my *The Building of the European Union* (Oxford, 3rd edn., 1998, 297 pp.), while more detailed than the present volume, is fairly accessible. An ampler academic introduction is Desmond Dinan's *Ever-Closer Union* (Basingstoke, 2nd edn., 1999, 596 pp.). A federalist view of the way in which the EU has developed is to be found in Michael Burgess, *Federalism and European Union: The Building of Europe, 1950–2000* (London, 2000, 290 pp.). Chapters on all the main policies are to be found in Helen Wallace and William Wallace (eds.), *Policy-Making in the European Union* (Oxford, 4th edn., 2000, 630 pp.). A wide range of subjects is also covered in Geoffrey Edwards and Georg Wiessala (eds.), *The European Union: Annual Review 1999/2000* (Oxford, 2000, 219 pp.). For the reader who does not aim at specialized knowledge, *Europe at the Dawn of the New Millennium* (Basingstoke, 1997, 229 pp.) by Enrique Baron Crespo, a former President of the European Parliament, is illuminating and readable.

Timothy Bainbridge, *The Penguin Companion to the European Union*

(Harmondsworth, 1999, 592 pp.) is an accurate and convenient **work of reference**.

For those who appreciate a **biographical** approach to the subject, the history of the EC up to the 1970s is seen through the eyes of its principal founding father in Jean Monnet's *Memoirs* (London, 1978, 544 pp.). Flavour and substance of the Delors period, from 1985 to 1994, are to be found in Charles Grant, *Inside the House that Jacques Built* (London, 1994, 305 pp.); and the political ideas and strategy of Delors are analysed in detail by George Ross in his *Jacques Delors and European Integration* (Cambridge, 1995). A range of leading actors in the uniting of Europe are given lively treatment in Martyn Bond, Julie Smith, and William Wallace (eds.), *Eminent Europeans* (London, 1996, 321 pp.). Hugo Young provides unsurpassed insights into the development of British relations with the EU, through chapters on a dozen British protagonists and antagonists from Churchill to Blair, in *This Blessed Plot* (Basingstoke, 1998, 558 pp.).

There is not much that is easy to read and gives a true and fair view of how the **institutions** work. Neill Nugent's *The Government and Politics of the European Union* (Basingstoke, 4th edn., 1999, 592 pp.) is reliable and comprehensive but not light reading. Shorter explanations of the institutions can be found in the chapter on 'Institutions or Constitution' in my *The Building of the European Union* and in Helen Wallace's chapter on 'The Institutions of the EU: Experience and Experiments' in Wallace and Wallace (eds.), *Policy-Making in the European Union* (both books cited above). Chapters 8–10 of Dinan's *Ever Closer Union* (also cited above) deal with 'The Commission', 'The European Council and the Council of Ministers', and 'The European Parliament'. Julie Smith's *Europe's Elected Parliament* (Sheffield, 1999, 198 pp.) is readable and informative. The literature on the Court of Justice and the Court of First Instance is mainly by the lawyers for the lawyers, but pp. 301–15 of Dinan's book offer a good summary.

Loukas Tsoukalis, in *The New European Economy Revisited: The Politics and Economics of Integration* (Oxford, 1997, 306 pp.), provides an enlightening overview of the field of **economics and economic policies**. Christopher Johnson's *In with the Euro, out with the Pound* (Harmondsworth, 1996, 256 pp.) argues for British participation and John Redwood's *Our Currency, Our Country: The Dangers of Monetary Union* (Harmondsworth, 1997, 214 pp.) argues against, while in Andrew Duff (ed.), *Understanding the Euro* (London, 1998, 160 pp.), a dozen authors discuss the various aspects. Lord Cockfield's *The European Union: Creating the Single Market* (Chichester, 1994, 185 pp.) is a lucid and entertaining account by the man who did most to create it, while Helen Wallace and Alasdair Young, in 'The Single Market' (chapter in Wallace and Wallace (eds.) *Policy-Making in the European Union*), bring you up to date. The budget is well explained by Iain Begg and Nigel Grimwade in *Paying for Europe* (Sheffield, 1998, 200 pp.), and the CAP by C. Ritson and D. R. Harvey (eds.) in *The Common Agricultural Policy* (Wallingford, Oxon., 2nd edn 1997, 448 pp.). Regional policies are covered in David Allen, 'Cohesion and the Structural Funds' (chapter in Wallace and Wallace (eds.), *Policy-Making in the European Union*). Ian Davidson analyses the argument about Anglo-Saxons and Rhinelanders in *Jobs and the Rhineland Model* (London, 1997, 80 pp.)

Useful annual summaries of the EU's **environmental policies** are given annually in Nigel Haig (ed.), *Manual of Environmental Policy: The EU and Britain* (Oxford: Elsevier Science), and in the *Environment Guide* of The EU Committee of the American Chamber of Commerce in Brussels.

Most of the recent literature on the EU's **external relations** is about the Common Foreign and Security Policy, though the external economic policies remain more effective and important. Simon Nuttall provides an authoritative overview in *European Foreign Policy* (Oxford, 2000, 280 pp.) and a variety of approaches to the CFSP are to be found in Martin Holland (ed.), *Common Foreign and Security Policy: The Record and Reforms* (London, 1997, 210pp.). Loukas Tsoukalis deals with the external economic policies in a chapter on 'European or Global Power' in his *The New European Economy Revisited* (cited above), including a section on the forthcoming enlargements. Well-informed books on the latter subject are Graham Avery and Fraser Cameron, *Enlargement of the European Union* (Sheffield, 1998, 198 pp.) and Heather Grabbe and Kirsty Hughes, *Enlarging the EU Eastwards: Prospects and Challenges* (London: 1998, 128 pp.), though events have moved fast since they were written.

The **Area of Freedom, Security and Justice** is also a fast-moving subject, in which the state of play in the first half of 2000 is to be found in Jörg Monar's chapter on 'Justice and Home Affairs', in Geoffrey Edwards and Georg Wiessala (eds.), *The European Union: Annual Review 1999/2000* (cited above).

Across the board the EU's website – http://europa.eu.int – is a vast quarry of information.

Chronology 1946–2000

25 March 1957	Rome Treaties establishing EEC and Euratom signed.
1 January 1958	Rome Treaties enter into force.

1960s

3 May 1960	Efta established by Austria, Denmark, Norway, Portugal, Sweden, Switzerland, UK.
14 December 1960	OEEC becomes OECD, including Canada and US as well as West European states.
31 July, 10 August 1961	Ireland, Denmark, UK apply to join Communities. Norway applies in April 1962.
14 January 1962	Common agricultural policy agreed by the Six.
14 January 1963	President de Gaulle terminates accession negotiations.
4 May 1964	Kennedy Round of Gatt negotiations begins with Community playing a leading part.
1 July 1965	France breaks off negotiations on financing CAP, boycotts Council until January 1966.
28–9 January 1966	Luxembourg 'Compromise' agreed. France returns to Council insisting on unanimity when 'very important' interests at stake.
11 May 1967	UK reactivates membership application, followed by Ireland, Denmark, Norway. De Gaulle still demurs.
1 July 1968	Customs union completed 18 months ahead of schedule.
1–2 December 1969	Community Summit agrees arrangements for financing CAP, and resumption of accession negotiations.

1970s

22 April 1970	Amending Treaty signed, giving Community all

	revenue from common external tariff and agricultural import levies plus share of value-added tax, and European Parliament some powers over budget.
30 June 1970	Negotiations for accession of Denmark, Ireland, Norway, UK begin.
27 October 1970	Council establishes 'EPC' procedures for foreign policy co-operation.
22 March 1971	Council adopts plan to achieve Emu by 1980, soon derailed by international monetary turbulence.
22 January 1972	Accession Treaties of Denmark, Ireland, Norway, UK signed (but Norwegians reject theirs in referendum).
1 January 1973	Denmark, Ireland, UK join Community.
9–10 December 1974	Paris Summit decides to hold meetings three times a year as European Council and gives go-ahead for direct elections to European Parliament.
28 February 1975	Community and 46 African, Caribbean, and Pacific countries sign Lomé Convention.
18 March 1975	European Regional Development Fund established.
12 June 1975	Greece applies to join.
22 July 1975	Amending Treaty signed, giving European Parliament more budgetary powers and setting up Court of Auditors.
1–2 December 1975	European Council takes formal decision for direct elections.
6 January 1977	New Commission takes office, Jenkins President.
28 March, 28 July 1977	Portugal, Spain apply to join.

7–8 April 1978	European Council endorses Joint Declaration of Parliament, Council, Commission, on fundamental rights.
4–5 December 1978	European Council establishes European Monetary System with Exchange Rate Mechanism based on ecu.
7, 10 June 1979	First direct elections to European Parliament.

1980s

1 January 1981	Greece becomes tenth member of Community.
14 February 1984	Draft Treaty on European Union, inspired by Spinelli, passed by big majority in European Parliament.
14, 17 June 1984	Second elections to European Parliament.
25–6 June 1984	European Council agrees on rebate to reduce UK's net contribution to Community budget.
7 January 1985	New Commission takes office, Delors President.
14 June 1985	Schengen Agreement eliminating border controls signed by Belgium, France, Germany, Luxembourg, Netherlands.
28–9 June 1985	European Council approves Commission project to complete single market by 1992; considers proposals from Parliament's Draft Treaty; initiates IGC for Treaty amendment.
2–4 December 1985	European Council agrees Single European Act.
1 January 1986	Spain, Portugal accede, membership now twelve.
17, 28 February 1986	Single European Act signed.
1 July 1987	Single European Act enters into force.
1 July 1988	Interinstitutional Agreement between Parliament, Council, Commission on budgetary discipline and procedure enters into force.
24 October 1988	Court of First Instance established.
15, 18 June 1989	Third elections to European Parliament.

17 July 1989	Austria applies to join.
9 November 1989	Fall of Berlin Wall. German Democratic Republic opens borders.
8–9 December 1989	European Council initiates IGC on Emu; all save UK adopt charter of workers' social rights.

1990s

28 April 1990	European Council agrees policy on German unification and relations with Central and East European states.
29 May 1990	Agreement signed to establish European Bank for Reconstruction and Development.
19 June 1990	Second Schengen Agreement signed.
20 June 1990	EEC and Efta start negotiations to create European Economic Area (EEA).
25–6 June 1990	European Council decides to call IGC on political union, parallel with that on Emu.
4, 16 July 1990	Cyprus, Malta apply to join.
3 October 1990	Unification of Germany.
14–15 December 1990	European Council launches IGCs on Emu and political union.
1 July 1991	Sweden applies to join.
9–10 December 1991	European Council agrees TEU (Maastricht Treaty).
16 December 1991	'Europe Agreements' with Poland, Hungary, Czechoslovakia signed; those with Czech Republic and Slovakia (successors to Czechoslovakia), Bulgaria, Estonia, Latvia, Lithunia, Romania, Slovenia follow at intervals.
7 February 1992	Maastricht Treaty signed.
18 March 1992	Finland applies to join.
2 May 1992	Agreement on EEA signed.
20 May 1992	Switzerland applies to join.
21 May 1992	CAP reform approved.

2 June 1992	Danish referendum rejects Maastricht Treaty.
14 September 1992	First ministerial meeting of participants in TACIS programme of assistance for CIS states.
20 September 1992	French referendum narrowly approves Maastricht Treaty.
25 November 1992	Norway applies to join.
6 December 1992	Swiss referendum rejects joining EEA; attempt to join EU shelved.
11–12 December 1992	European Council offers Denmark special arrangements to facilitate Treaty ratification; endorses Delors package of budgetary proposals; agrees to start accession negotiations with Austria, Norway, Sweden, Finland.
31 December 1992	Bulk of single market legislation completed on time.
18 May 1993	Second Danish referendum accepts Maastricht Treaty.
21–2 June 1993	European Council declares associated Central and East European states can join when they fulfil the political and economic conditions.
1 November 1993	Maastricht Treaty enters into force.
5 December 1993	Commission adopts White Paper on growth, competitiveness, employment.
9–10 March 1994	Committee of Regions, set up by Maastricht Treaty, holds inaugural session.
31 March, 5 April 1994	Hungary, Poland apply to join.
9, 12 June 1994	Fourth elections to European Parliament.
15 July 1994	European Council nominates Santer to succeed Delors as Commission President.
28 November 1994	Norwegian referendum rejects accession.
1 January 1995	Austria, Finland, Sweden join, membership now fifteen.

12 July 1995	European Parliament appoints first Union Ombudsman.
26 July 1995	Member states sign Europol Convention.
27–8 November 1995	Euro-Mediterranean Conference in Barcelona.
31 December 1995	EC–Turkey customs union enters into force.
29 March 1996	IGC to revise Maastricht Treaty begins.
16 July 1997	Commission presents 'Opinions' on applications of ten Central and East European countries, and 'Agenda 2000' proposals to adapt EU policies for enlargement.
2 October 1997	Amsterdam Treaty signed.
12 March 1998	Accession negotiations open with Cyprus, Czech Republic, Estonia, Hungary, Poland, Slovenia.
3 May 1998	Council decides eleven states ready to adopt euro on 1 January 1999.
1 June 1998	European Central Bank established.
24–5 October 1998	European Council agrees measures of defence co-operation.
31 December 1998	Council fixes irrevocable conversion rates between euro and currencies of participating states.
1 January 1999	Euro becomes official currency of Austria, Belgium, Finland, France, Germany, Ireland, Italy, Luxembourg, Netherlands, Portugal, Spain.
15 March 1999	Commission resigns following report by independent committee on allegations of mismanagement and fraud.
24 March 1999	Prodi nominated new Commission President.
24–5 March 1999	European Council agrees on Agenda 2000.
1 May 1999	Amsterdam Treaty enters into force.
10–13 June 1999	Fifth elections to European Parliament.

| 10–11 December 1999 | European Council decides on accession negotiations with six more states; recognizes Turkey as applicant; initiates IGC for Treaty revision. |

2000

15 January 2000	Accession negotiations open with Bulgaria, Latvia, Lithuania, Malta, Romania, Slovakia.
14 February 2000	IGC begins.
1 March 2000	Commission adopts White Paper on its reform.
3 May 2000	Commission proposes Greece to become twelfth member of euro-zone.
9 May 2000	European Institutions celebrate 50th anniversary of Schuman Declaration.
20 June 2000	European Council agrees measures for flexibility in EU economy.
23 June 2000	Lomé Convention V signed.
7–10 December 2000	European Council concludes negotiations for Nice Treaty and welcomes Charter of Fundamental Rights.

Glossary

Words in *italics* refer to other entries.

Accession: The process of joining the *European Union*. After accession treaties have been negotiated, all member states must ratify them and the European Parliament must give its assent.

Acquis Communautaire: The full set of the *European Union*'s legislative, regulatory, judicial, and normative output.

Agenda 2000: Measures to reform *common agricultural* and *cohesion policies* with a view to enlargement to Central and Eastern Europe.

Amsterdam Treaty: See *Treaty of Amsterdam*.

Area of Freedom, Security and Justice (AFSJ): The *Amsterdam Treaty* incorporated the *Schengen Agreements* in the *European Community*, providing for abolition of frontier controls; free movement of people; judicial and police co-operation against cross-border crime. Ireland, the UK, and to some extent Denmark opted out of the abolition of frontier controls and of the aspects involving EC institutions.

Asymmetric shocks: Affect different regions within an economy in different ways: a potential problem for the euro-zone.

Barriers to trade: Tariffs and quotas have been eliminated from trade among member states. The aim of the single market, to eliminate the non-tariff barriers, has been largely achieved, though some still remain.

Budget of the *European Union*: Revenue comes from *own resources*; two-thirds of spending is on the *common agricultural* and *cohesion* policies.

Citizenship: The *Treaty on European Union* created a European citizenship, alongside member states' citizenships. Citizens are entitled to rights conferred by the treaties.

Cohesion policy: The *European Union*'s regional development policy, implemented through *structural funds* accounting for one-third of European Union *budget* spending.

Comitology: System of committees of member states' officials supervising the *Commission's* work on behalf of the *Council*.

Commission, European Commission: The main executive body of the *European Union*, comprising twenty Commissioners, responsible for different policy areas. In addition to its executive functions, the Commission initiates legislation and supervises compliance. The term 'Commission' is often used collectively for the Commission and its staff of some 16,000.

Committee of Permanent Representatives (Coreper): See *Council*.

Committee of the Regions: Comprises representatives of regional and local authorities. Provides opinions on legislation and issues reports on its own initiative.

Common agricultural policy (CAP): Supports agriculture through subsidies and other price support mechanisms, accounting for almost half the *European Union*'s budget spending. Reforms have moved towards direct support for farmers and lower price supports.

Common Foreign and Security Policy (CFSP): Second *pillar* of the *European Union*, for intergovernmental co-operation on foreign policy and, using the capacities of *Western European Union*, defence. The Secretary-General of the *Council* is also the 'High Representative' who assists the Council *Presidency* in representing the European Union externally.

Community: See *European Community*.

Compulsory Expenditure (CE): Budgetary expenditure, largely for the *common agricultural policy*, over which the *Council* has more power than the *European Parliament*.

Co-operation in Justice and Home Affairs (CJHA): Former third *pillar* of the *European Union*, for co-operation relating to movement of people across frontiers and for combating cross-frontier crime. The *Treaty of Amsterdam* transferred much of the CJHA into the *Community's* new *Area of Freedom, Security and Justice*. Since Ireland and UK opted out of AFSA, a reduced third pillar for *Police and Judicial Co-operation in Criminal Matters* remains.

Council, Council of Ministers: Comprises representatives of member states at ministerial level. It amends and *votes* on legislation, supervises execution of *Community* policies, and is responsible for policies under the second and third *pillars*. It is supported by the Council Secretariat in Brussels, and by the Committee of Permanent Representatives and its system of committees (see *comitology*). The Council, with the *European Council*, is the *European Union's* most powerful political institution.

Court of First Instance: Judges cases in areas such as competition law and disputes between the institutions and their employees.

Court of Justice: The final judicial authority with respect to *Community* law. Its fifteen judges, one from each member state sitting in Luxembourg, have developed an extensive case-law (see *European legal order*). The Court has ensured that the rule of law prevails in the Community.

Direct effect: See *European legal order*.

Directive: A *Community* legal act that is 'binding, as to the result to be achieved', but leaves to member states' authorities 'the choice of form and methods'.

Economic and Monetary Union (Emu): Twelve member states are participating in Emu, having satisfied the 'convergence criteria' of sound finance and irrevocably fixed their exchange rates with the euro. The euro replaces their currencies at the beginning of 2002. Monetary policy is the responsibility of the *European Central Bank* and the *European System of Central Banks*. There is a system for co-ordination of economic policy.

Economic and Social Committee (Ecosoc): Comprises representatives of employers, workers, and social groups. Provides opinions on *European Community* legislation and issues reports on its own initiative.

Electoral systems: In elections to the *European Parliament*, proportional representation is now used in all countries, since UK adopted it for the 1999 elections.

Enhanced co-operation: Allows those states that want to integrate more closely than others in particular fields to do so within the *European Union* framework.

European Atomic Energy Community (Euratom): Established in 1957 alongside the *European Economic Community* to promote co-operation in the field of atomic energy; undertakes research and development for civilian purposes.

European Central Bank (ECB): Responsible for monetary policy for the euro-zone. Based in Frankfurt, the ECB is run by an Executive Board. Its members and the Governors of central banks in the euro-zone comprise ECB's Governing Council. ECB and central banks together form the European System of Central Banks (ESCB), whose primary objective is to maintain price stability. None of these participants may take instructions from any other body.

European Coal and Steel Community (ECSC): Launched by the Schuman Declaration of 9 May 1950, placing coal and steel sectors of six states (Belgium, France, Germany, Italy, Luxembourg, Netherlands) under a system of common governance. The *European Economic Community* and *Euratom* were based on the ECSC's institutional structure.

European Commission: See *Commission*.

European Community (EC): The EC is the central *pillar* of the *European Union*. Incorporating the *European Economic Community*, the *European Coal and Steel Community*, and *Euratom*, it contains federal elements of the *European Union* institutions and is responsible for the bulk of European Union activities.

European Convention on Human Rights and Fundamental Freedoms: A framework for the protection of human rights across Europe, adopted in 1950 by the Council of Europe. *European Union* states are all signatories and it is a basis for the respect of human rights in the European Union.

European Council: Comprises the Prime Ministers of the member states, Presidents of Finland and France (who have some executive functions), and President of the *Commission*. Takes decisions that require resolution or impetus at that level and defines political guidelines for the *European Union*.

European Court of Justice (ECJ): See *Court of Justice*.

European Defence Community (EDC): A bold attempt in the early 1950s to integrate the armed forces of the *European Coal and Steel Community* states, shelved by the French National Assembly.

European Economic Community (EEC): Established in 1958 by the *Treaty of Rome*, its competences included the creation of a common market among the six member states and wide-ranging economic policy co-operation. Its main institutions were the *Commission*, *Council*, *European Parliament*, *Court of Justice*. It is the basis for today's *European Community*.

European legal order: The *Court of Justice* has established key principles of Community law. One is 'direct effect', enabling individuals to secure their rights under Community law in the same way as member states' laws. Another is 'primacy' of Community law, ensuring it is evenly applied throughout the Community.

European Monetary System (EMS): A precursor of *Economic and Monetary Union*, its key element was the Exchange Rate Mechanism, limiting exchange rate fluctuations.

European Parliament (EP): The directly elected body of the *European Union*, its *Members* (MEPs) have substantial powers over *legislation*, the *budget*, and the *Commission*.

European Political Co-operation (EPC): Intergovernmental foreign policy co-operation, introduced in 1970 and replaced in 1993 by the *Common Foreign and Security Policy*.

European System of Central Banks (ESCB): See *European Central Bank*.

European Union (EU): Created by the *Treaty on European Union*, with two new *pillars* alongside the central *Community* pillar, for co-operation in foreign policy and in 'justice and home affairs'. While the three pillars share common institutions, the two new ones are predominantly intergovernmental.

Federation: A federal polity is one in which the functions of government are divided between democratic institutions at two or more levels. The powers are usually divided according to the principle of *subsidiarity*, the member states or constituent parts having those powers that they can manage effectively.

Free movement: The treaties provide for free movement within the *European Union* of people, goods, capital, and services, known as 'the four freedoms'.

Intergovernmental Conference (IGC): The main way in which the *European Union*'s treaties are revised. Member states' representatives in the IGC draft an amending treaty, which must be ratified by each state before it enters into force.

Legislative procedures: Most *European Community* laws are enacted under the co-decision procedure, giving both *European Parliament* and *Council* powers to accept, amend, or reject legislation. The co-operation procedure, which gave the EP less power, is no longer important; but the consultation procedure, where EP is merely informed of Council's intentions, is still quite widely applicable. The assent procedure gives EP powers over accession treaties, association agreements, and some legislative matters.

Maastricht Treaty: See *Treaty on European Union*.

Members of the European Parliament (MEPs): Currently 625 MEPs are elected to the *European Parliament* from across the member states. MEPs represent their constituents; scrutinize legislation in committees; vote on laws and the budget; supervise the *Commission*; debate the range of *European Union* affairs.

Nice Treaty: *See* Treaty of Nice.

Non-compulsory expenditure (NCE): Expenditure over which the *European Parliament* has more power than the *Council*, currently around half the total *budget*.

North Atlantic Treaty Organisation (Nato): Founded in 1949, it is the security umbrella for Western Europe, tying in the US to the European security system.

Own resources: The tax revenue for the *budget of the European Union*. The main sources are percentages of member states' GNPs and of the base for value-added tax; smaller amounts come from external tariffs and agricultural import levies.

Permanent representations: Each member state has a permanent representation in Brussels, which is a centre for its interaction with the *European Union*. The head of the representation is the state's representative in Coreper (see *Council*).

PHARE: Assistance for the process of transformation in Central and Eastern Europe.

Pillars: The *Maastricht Treaty* set up the *European Union* using a pillar system. Each pillar is relatively autonomous, though linked to the other pillars by a set of common provisions. The central pillar is the *European Community* and the other two are for the *Common Foreign and Security*

Policy and *Co-operation in Justice and Home Affairs*, since renamed Police and Judicial Co-operation in Criminal Matters.

Police and Judicial Co-operation in Criminal Matters: See *Co-operation in Justice and Home Affairs*.

Presidency: The *Council* and *European Council* are chaired by representatives of one of the member states, on a six-month rotating basis. The President-in-Office also heads the representation of the *European Union* under the *Common Foreign and Security Policy* and helps to set the direction of the EU for that period.

Primacy: See *European legal order*.

Qualified majority voting (QMV): See *voting*.

Regulation: A *European Community* legal act that is 'binding in its entirety and directly applicable' in all member states.

Schengen Agreements: Originating in 1985 outside the *European Union*, the Schengen Agreements now cover all member states save Ireland, the UK, and to some extent Denmark. The Agreements have been incorporated in the *European Community* (see *Area of Freedom, Security and Justice*).

Secondary legislation: Laws enacted by the institutions within the powers given them by the treaties.

Single European Act (SEA): Signed in 1986, the first major reform of the Rome Treaty. It provided for the 1992 programme to complete the single market; added some new competences; extended the use of qualified majority *voting*; enhanced the role of the *European Parliament*.

Structural funds: Cohesion Fund, Guidance section of the European

Agricultural Guarantee and Guidance Fund, Regional Development Fund, Social Fund (see *cohesion policy*).

Subsidiarity: A principle requiring action to be taken at *European Union* level only when it can be more effective than action by individual states.

TACIS (Technical Assistance to the Commonwealth of Independent States): Assistance for the process of transformation in CIS states.

Treaties of Rome: See *European Economic Community* and *European Atomic Energy Community*. The EEC Treaty is often called 'the Treaty of Rome'.

Treaty of Amsterdam: Signed in 1997, it extended the scope of co-decision and reformed the *pillars* on foreign policy and on justice and home affairs.

Treaty of Nice: Concluded by *European Council* in December 2000. It aims to prepare the institutions for the forthcoming enlargement, somewhat extends the scope for *qualified majority voting*, and facilitates *enhanced co-operation*.

Treaty on European Union (TEU): Signed in 1991 at Maastricht, it established the *European Union*. It laid down the procedures for creating *Economic and Monetary Union*; gave *European Parliament* important new powers; introduced a European *citizenship*; set up two new *pillars*, for *common foreign and security policy* and *co-operation in justice and home affairs*.

Union: See *European Union*.

Voting: Most *Council* decisions are now taken by qualified majority voting (QMV), giving each state a number of votes related to its population but weighted in favour of smaller states. The total number of votes is 87, and 62 constitute a qualified majority. To provide for enlargement, new weighting is to be introduced as from 2005. The unanimity procedure applies less frequently to *Community* legislation but is prevalent in the other two *pillars*. Voting by simple majority is limited mainly to procedural matters.

Western European Union (WEU): Created in 1954 by the UK and *European Community* member states. After a long period of inaction, the *Maastricht* and *Amsterdam* Treaties provided for links between the *European Union* and WEU, which is being incorporated into the EU and developed as a European arm of *Nato*. Most members of EU are members of WEU.

World Trade Organisation (WTO): The 1995 successor to Gatt, WTO regulates international trade. It aims to reduce barriers to international trade and has mechanisms for resolving disputes.

Index

Page references in *italics* indicate illustrations and their captions.

Index

Index

Expand your collection of
VERY SHORT INTRODUCTIONS

Visit the
VERY SHORT INTRODUCTIONS
Web site

www.oup.co.uk/vsi

➤ **Information** about all published titles

➤ News of **forthcoming books**

➤ **Extracts** from the books, including titles not yet published

➤ **Reviews** and views

➤ **Links** to other **web sites** and main OUP web page

➤ Information about **VSIs in translation**

➤ **Contact** the editors

➤ **Order** other **VSIs** on-line